Tiny Kitchen Feast

Introduction ~ **pix**
Kitchen Essentials ~ **pxiv**

Breakfast & Brunch

Masa Cakes Benedict with Smoked Tofu, Refried Black Beans & Chimichurri Rojo 🥜~ **p2**

Sweet Risotto with Plantains & Orange Amaretto Sauce ~ **p4**

Guava-Stuffed French Toast with Coconut Syrup ~ **p10**

Stewed Banana Oatmeal 🥜~ **p11**

Loaded Potato Pancakes ~ **p12**

Chilaquiles: Tortillas in a Chili Simmering Sauce 🥜~ **p15**

Handhelds, Salads & Soups

Tempura-Fried Squash Tacos with Sweet Corn Crema, Tamarind BBQ Sauce & Orange Sesame Slaw 🥜~ **p20**

Seitan Philly ~ **p22**

Tamarind Guava BBQ Tempeh Sandwiches 🥜~ **p26**

C.B.L.T.: Coconut Bacon, Lettuce & Tomato Sandwich with Aji Amarillo Aioli 🥜~ **p27**

Superfood Salad with Smoky Tahini Beetroot Vinaigrette 🥜~ **p32**

Nat's Ultimate Burritos ~ **p36**

Napa Cabbage & Orange Salad with Chili Pepitas & Creamy Guava Vinaigrette 🥜~ **p37**

Grilled Romaine Lettuce, Charred Tomato, Green Chili Croutons & Manchego Dressing 🥜🥥~ **p38**

Chanterelle & Hazelnut Ramen 🥜~ **p40**

Coconut Soup with Pistachio Pesto 🥜🥜~ **p45**

Peanut Stew with Sweet Potato, Peppers & Coconut Milk 🥜🥜~ **p47**

Contents

Appetizers

Coconut Fry Bread ~ **p50**

Baked Cabbage Rolls with Picadillo &
Aji Amarillo Corn Crema 🌾 ~ **p52**

Empanetzels with Soyrizo &
Sweet Plantain ~ **p53**

Guacamole with Caramelized Ginger
& Orange 🌾 ~ **p55**

Roasted Strawberry Bruschetta
with Pesto Butter & Strawberry
Balsamic Glaze 🌾 🥜 ~ **p56**

Main Staples

Creamy Ramen Noodles ~ **p62**

Plantain Gnocchi with Meat-Free
Mushroom Carnitas ~ **p63**

Smoked Poblano & Manchego
Mac 'n' Cheese 🌿 ~ **p64**

Creamy Butternut Squash Pasta, Coconut
Bacon & Gingersnap Crumble ~ **p66**

Some Kinda Jumbled Jambalaya ~ **p70**

Coconut Braised Black-Eyed Peas 🌾 ~ **p71**

Arroz Mamposteao: Puerto Rican Stewed
Beans & Rice 🌾 ~ **p72**

Braised Kale with Coconut Milk &
Tahini 🌾 ~ **p75**

Yucca Frites with Charred Scallion
Aioli 🌾 ~ **p76**

Tostones/Maduros 🌾 ~ **p78**

Hearty Proteins

Soyrizo 🌾 ~ **p84**

Simple Seitan ~ **p87**

Hibiscus Flower Birria Tacos 🌾 ~ **p88**

Coconut Bacon 🌾 ~ **p94**

Mushroom Carnitas 🌾 ~ **p96**

Picadillo "Beefy" Stew with Raisins &
Green Olives 🌾 ~ **p97**

Albóndigas Guisadas: No-Meat Meatballs
Stewed in Sofrito ~ **p98**

Campfire Eats

Whole Roasted Cauliflower with Garlic &
Creamy Chipotle Sauce 🌾 ~ **p104**

Sexy 'Shrooms ~ **p107**

Twice-Cooked Fingerling Potatoes with
Charred Scallion Aioli 🌾 ~ **p110**

Nachos with Soyrizo & Smoky Poblano
Queso 🌾 ~ **p113**

Grilled Tempeh Kabobs with Miso Plum
Glaze 🌾 ~ **p118**

Drinks

Saffron Pineapple Lemonade 🌾 ~ **p122**

Aguave Limonada 🌾 ~ **p124**

Sweet Corn Drink 🌾 ~ **p125**

Avocado Coquito with Miso Caramel 🌾 ~ **p126**

Golden Milk Tea 🌾 ~ **p130**

Sauces, Butters & Seasonings

Queso 🌾 ~ **p136**

Sofrito 🌾 ~ **p139**

Poblano Aioli 🌾 ~ **p143**

Aji Amarillo Aioli 🌾 ~ **p143**

Charred Scallion Aioli 🌾 ~ **p144**

Chimichurri Rojo 🌾 ~ **p146**

Mock Mole 🌾 ~ **p148**

Sun-Dried Tomato Butter 🌾 ~ **p149**

Caramelized Scallion Butter 🌾 ~ **p150**

Nikki Mix 🌾 ~ **p152**

Annatto Oil 🌾 ~ **p152**

Annatto and Orange Butter 🌾 ~ **p155**

Index ~ **p158**

Acknowledgments ~ **p164**

About the Author ~ **p165**

VEGETARIAN

GLUTEN FREE

CONTAINS NUTS

Sustenance

I simmer in the process. Music sets a tone. I sharpen my knife and let the lyrics flood in, propelling my hands to perform. I organically pick up ingredients, sometimes based on color, other times based on a centralized idea. I lay out my cutting board. I let a million things rush through my head and then I let my heart flush them all away.

It's magnetic once the beat hits in my headphones. My body naturally sways, my knife is the extension of my energy, like when I put pen to paper. I lose the need to know the conclusion of the art, once I've entered into a flowstate. Sometimes I'm so out of body, I become the knife, I become the balance of flavor, I become the flame of the cooktop. My food is my love letter, my method is my dance. I am not separate from my creation.

Then, I place the food in front of you. That's when I snap back. That's when I notice your reaction. That's the moment the universe syncs, celebrating human connection in its full capacity. To know me is to know that moment is my ultimate high.

As you journey through this book, I hope you feel a bit closer to me and my purpose. I hope you get the sense that the food is a culmination of my dharma. I am beyond grateful to be able to spread love and humility through cuisine. Enjoy.

"Growing up, I spent most of my free time in the kitchen of my grandmother, Matilde."

Growing up, I spent most of my free time in the kitchen of my grandmother, Matilde. Apart from when I got a little bit of video gaming in when my cousins weren't hogging the Super Nintendo, I was sitting on the kitchen countertop, observing Matilde in her element.

Upon entering her space, you had to go through these double doors that looked like they were straight out of a western saloon. You were then welcomed by the warm light flooding through the bay window at the opposite end, home to a variety of cacti. You could often hear the sharpening of knives as my grandmother honed them on the honing steel. I found that sound so soothing because it signaled that culinary magic was about to happen. I admired her dearly. She was the ultimate woman: wife to a military husband and mother to four children, who moved to the U.S. from Puerto Rico in the 1930s. She was a dancer, an artist. To me, she was a woman who signified beauty and grace. I split my time between my mom's house and hers and would be so excited when I got to eat her food. Rice and beans were always available. It's the staple I remember most fondly and the dish in this book that holds the most sentiment. While most kids ate potato chips as a snack, I ate tostones (fried plantains). When it came to sweets, my dessert of choice was flan, a silky custard. I haven't eaten it much since she passed but it was a flavor I associate with her love, decadent and rich.

I barely remember a time when she wasn't preparing something. While we ate breakfast, lunch was discussed; while lunch was consumed, dinner was in the works. She was the glue that held the family together for the holidays. We all gathered at her house and we never went hungry.

I credit my grandmother with my affinity for cooking and my desire to make it my career. As well as spending a lot of time in the kitchen with her, I endlessly watched cooking shows. Fast forward almost a decade and I was cooking meals for friends who told me I had a knack for it. Shortly after, I began working in the food and beverage industry. I graduated from the Culinary Institute of Charleston in 2013 and got my first cooking job at a sports bar while I studied. I remember applying for the job and the manager telling me he wanted me to work as a server. I'm sure it was because of my looks, but I had to assert myself and tell him I was a student in culinary school and wanted to work as a cook. Even though I had no experience, I had to test the waters known as the BOH, or back of house. I quickly worked my way up and started running the kitchen by myself most nights.

From there, I moved to working at a more refined Italian restaurant. They started me at the appetizer station but, after just a week, I was bumped up to the hot line, quickly working my way to every station: pasta, fry, sauté, grill. I vividly remember working the grill station one day.

Enjoying a beautiful day outside of **Death Valley National Park**

I had never worked with such expensive proteins, let alone run a grill station. I had to cook a porterhouse. A porterhouse steak can be more than 40 oz (1.1 kg) of meat and contains two different cuts, one a strip and the other a tenderloin. This means that each side of the steak requires separate cook times to achieve the overall cook the customer has asked for. It's an art to grill a porterhouse correctly and I had only been on the grill station a few days. It was the most expensive thing on the menu.

The chef had unwavering confidence in me so he didn't give me much guidance. He just told me not to move the steak until I felt it was time to flip it. I had no idea what that meant but I had learned how to test the doneness by touch. I went with my gut, relying on the knowledge I'd acquired from school, and put it on the plate. I'm pretty sure I held my breath while the steak made its way to the diner's table. Apparently, this was a VIP customer. I went about my work but I was so nervous.

Twenty minutes later, the front-of-house manager came charging through the door. He was a tall, lanky man who looked straight out of the mafia. With a loud New York accent, he bellowed, "Who cooked the steak for table yada yada?!" With hesitation and dread, I slowly raised my hand. He looked at me and said (...drumroll please...) "Cooked to perfection!" I don't think I'd ever been more proud of myself. From then on, I cooked at multiple restaurants in Charleston, always taking a leadership role. But while I performed well during those ten-plus years in the industry, I was getting burned out.

I met my wife, Abi, and after one trip west, my mind started wandering and travel came to the forefront of my thoughts. Working in the food and beverage industry was such a tedious grind. My work had become less about my love for food and more about the paycheck, scraping to

My wife Abi and I enjoying an enchanting forest walk in Sequoia National Park

Making homemade
vegetable stock
over a campfire for
my Chanterelle and
Hazelnut Ramen

get by, long hours, and getting to the bar after work. It was simply the culture. In my 31 years, to that point, I hadn't really been beyond the southeast. My spirit was longing for a change. I still loved to cook, but the idea of seeing the world became more persistent. Then I found the #vanlife hashtag on Instagram.

But let me back up five years, before taking off on our maiden voyage. When I was living in James Island, South Carolina, my roommate met this man one night and invited him back to our place for a drink. When he arrived in his bright yellow VW bus, with his well-traveled dog, I couldn't wait to talk to him. I felt that it was the perfect night to pop the 1996 magnum Barolo wine I had taken from that Italian restaurant that had kick-started my career. We sat in his van and talked about his life. He was from Canada and had traveled all over, taking pictures of his dog in different landscapes. Now, he even has books featuring his dog in the landscape—kind of like a canine *Where's Waldo?*—and has exploded on social media. He was doing the #vanlife lifestyle before it became a hashtag. I still felt very much indebted to the food and beverage industry but that night, and our conversation, never left my mind.

Fast forward to the year before we took off in the van. One day, I turned to Abi and asked her thoughts about living in a van and traveling indefinitely. Without hesitation, she was all in. She started doing research before I could really consider what I'd asked, and we spent that year working extra jobs, finding our vehicle, building it out, getting married, and preparing for the open road. It was all happening so quickly and I remember my co-workers being confused about what we were doing. I would drive the van to work and, little by little, they watched its transformation.

This lifestyle was kind of a foreign concept to people working normal jobs and living the typical "American dream." I had always been one to go against the grain, never really fitting in and always interested in less mainstream pursuits. The more we got done on the van, the more our friends and acquaintances were intrigued. Now, most of those people who were skeptical at first, including our parents, follow us on social media and are among our biggest fans.

That first year on the road was spectacular. Abi and I considered it our extended honeymoon. We were seeing and experiencing all these new places while being elated by our recent marriage. Once we got into a groove with the very different processes that come with living in a mobile vehicle, I started to consider how I could continue to share my love of cooking. After all, it was my passion and I didn't want it simmering on the back burner. I mean, sure, I was making elaborate dinners for us, but my goal was to figure out how to extend that love language to the masses.

We had started a YouTube channel when we hit the road as a way to share our travels with friends and family, and as a way to remember it all ourselves, later. After that first year, we started doing a second video a week, focusing on my cooking. We called it the "Let's Play, Ride, and Eat" series. (Our YouTube is called "Let's Play, Ride, and Seek," so we thought it was catchy.) This allowed me to make food, share recipes, and create a foundation for wherever my passion would lead next. I always just saw it as a stepping stone and a chance to lean into my silly personality while having my own cooking show, just like those I had watched all those years ago. It felt like I'd come full circle, having my wife as the filmmaker and editor, allowing me to solely focus on the food and creating dishes. We made a great team but, after about a year, it was becoming too much to put two videos a week out on the channel.

Once again, I found myself a bit lost: I wanted to cook but longed to have it reach beyond our van table. One of the most valuable experiences I had was doing a pop-up restaurant on the beach in Baja California Sur, Mexico. Abi and I had traveled there the winter before Covid-19 hit and it was our favorite place we'd traveled to. We spent over a month at one beach and met a couple who asked us to create menus and do a pop-up kitchen. I was so excited at the opportunity and for four weeks, we did just that, devising a new concept every week and inviting surfers and beachgoers to enjoy meals we'd prepared out of our van.

It was quite the hit, and we did different fusion menus that were prepared and cooked around a fire just steps from the ocean. In all my years in the industry, I felt most aligned with my craft during that month. I was creating recipes from pure passion, inspired by the Baja California Sur, Mexico area. Our friends were so motivating and our ideas all meshed in this symbiotic way. I'll never forget that experience and owe that to several of the dishes that made it into this book.

That brings us to how this book came about. It is the culmination of all these formative years. I wanted to learn how to keep cooking for people on the road. Several TV shows reached out to us, interested in our minimal travel lifestyle, and even a cooking show. But none of them seemed right in our hearts. Knowing that I also loved to write, I had an aha moment when I thought about combining food and writing. And here we are.

I hope you can find more than just recipes in these pages. Whether it is a connection to your own nostalgia, inspiration to hit the road, or a desire to pursue your ultimate passions and live your life in a way that lights your soul on fire, let the book speak to you. It took me years to find my voice and to truly acknowledge my yearning for an alternative lifestyle. Once I dove into the unknown, I found it to be a safe haven. It kick-started a life I couldn't have imagined from the starting line.

These recipes are a part of a vivid process of self-discovery that emerged through the destinations that inspired them. I hope you see them as a stepping stone to creating your own unique dishes, and as a way to facilitate beautiful memories with the people who mean the most to you.

This is the first time I've written recipes down as I've always followed my grandmother's style and allowed intuition to drive my art. It was quite a challenge for me to sit and put measurements to my art, but I hope you can feel my determination to deliver a well-rounded set of recipes from my tiny kitchen to yours.

My friend Joaquin and I making gnocchi for a pop-up dinner on the beach in Baja California Sur, Mexico

I encourage you to remix these recipes. They are all simply templates to riff off. To me, that's the ultimate way to cook.

Coconut milk, orange, sofrito, garlic, agave, and onion are staples in many of these recipes. I have an affinity for these ingredients: they are my spirit ingredients and elements of my love language.

This book is mostly plant-based, with a few vegetarian recipes, too. Any time I refer to milk, butter, cheese, mayonnaise, and so on, I'm using vegan versions. But I'm not here to limit you so feel free to alter the recipes to suit your way of eating. I am simply creating a foundation of flavor for you to build upon. For any recipes using plant proteins, feel free to replace with actual meat substitutes if you wish. If you want to use steak instead of tempeh, please go ahead.

I have always considered cooking to be a creative outlet, so following a recipe to the T is not my style. Neither do I expect it to be yours. Have fun with the recipes! Email me at letsplayrideandseek@gmail.com if you think of a cool substitute or addition. Food is a gateway to community and a way to open a conversation. It is a vehicle for bringing people together and a way to find joy in something we all do daily. My hope is that the uniqueness of the recipes will help spark a creative flow and a zest for cooking and good food.

"I encourage you to remix these recipes. They are all simply templates to riff off. To me, that's the ultimate way to cook."

Kitchen Essentials

All creatives have items that are vital to our craft. Whether they are necessary for execution, hold sentimental value, or just add to our own unique styles, they are our tools for success. Since I made the transition from commercial and home kitchens to a moving vehicle with much less space, I have had to get creative with how I cook and some of my tools. Here are a few of my essentials that are ideal for smaller cooking spaces, as well as for life on the road.

Tools

 My chef's knife My knife is an extension of my arm. I cut, chop, mince, smash, hone, sharpen, admire, and just look hella cool with this item. My favorite knife is my hand-crafted steel chef's knife by Feral Forge.

 Tortilla press You'll need a T-press to make your own tortillas or to smash plantains with ease. Having one has been a game changer for me.

 Steamer Bamboo steamers are cheap and versatile. I use mine to keep my homemade tortillas warm and to steam veggies or dumplings while boiling pasta or making rice. Plus, it's easy to store and clean up and won't break easily.

 A really good non-stick pan These are essential for easy clean up. Most of us on the road have gray tanks, where our sink water diverts to, and the smell (even if you only cook vegan) is intense. Wiping out food before washing the dishes helps and having non-stick pans makes cleaning super easy. Plus, who doesn't like flipping a pancake with ease?

 Collapsible cookware When storage is limited, pots with fold-down handles and strainers or other containers that can be made smaller are ideal for fitting into nooks and crannies.

 Tongs Another extension of my hand. If you're cooking over an open fire (which I suggest for some of these recipes), tongs will be your friend, too.

Ingredients

 Kosher salt Everyone laughs when I enter their home kitchens to cook, look around for salt, and am (usually) disappointed to only find iodized or pink Himalayan salt. I use kosher salt. Because it is coarser, I can evenly distribute it much easier. I can also use it to cure fruits and vegetables. Unless I'm baking (which you won't find me doing very often), I stay away from iodized salt. As far as I'm concerned, this was the salt used in the old days when people didn't salt during cooking but passed it around the table, hoping to add some last-minute flavor to bland food. What a nightmare! Instead, salt in stages; salt as you cook. If you don't salt as you go, you won't pull out the nuances of flavor. Pink Himalayan salt is lovely, but it's for finishing dishes or salting avocados or tomatoes for a salad.

Liquid aminos This is another way to add umami to plant-based dishes. It also has less salt and is gluten free, in contrast to its close relative, soy sauce, which can sometimes contain gluten.

Corn masa When visiting Baja California Sur, Mexico, I fell in love with fresh corn tortillas. Now I can't do without this item.

Beans I grew up on beans. My kitchen is always stocked up. Whether dried or canned, beans are versatile, cheap, and can take on just about any flavor.

Citrus Fresh citrus enhances the flavor of anything. You can use the juice and the zest to really take flavors up a notch. You'll see I use fresh orange in most of my recipes. I'm obsessed.

Fresh herbs These are another way to pack in a lot of flavor. The addition of fresh herbs at the end of the cooking process adds such a vibrant, fresh explosion of flavor to almost any meal. Cilantro (coriander), thyme, and rosemary, as well as scallions (spring onions), are some of my favorites.

Tahini Whether thickening a sauce, adding nuttiness to a stew, or creating a sexy dressing, tahini has so many uses. Check out the stewed kale recipe and see if you can taste the flavor this pureed sesame seed paste brings to the table.

Rice Probably the ingredient I eat the most, rice was the base to most of my meals growing up. There are many varieties and cooking styles.

A neutral oil with a high smoke point
I tend to cook at a higher heat as I like to deglaze dishes (add a liquid to a pan to release the browned bits) and caramelize ingredients to add that umami flavor. Therefore, I need an oil with a high smoke point, which won't add any competing flavors. Vegetable, canola, avocado, and pure olive oils are great choices that won't burn during high-heat cooking. The last thing you want is for your pan to catch on fire from your oil.

Nutritional yeast This is an essential item of vegan cooking, in my opinion. If you want umami, cheesy flavor goodness, look no further. I refer to this staple as "nootch" throughout the book as it's easier (and sounds cooler). Plus, it's gluten free!

Agave I simply prefer using agave over sugar in most applications. It is less refined than sugar and has a lighter flavor than maple or brown rice syrup. It adds sweetness without changing the flavor profile of the dish. (If I do use sugar, I use organic cane sugar to avoid less-than-ideal processing practices.)

Liquid smoke This is a great way to add a natural smoky flavor to vegan or vegetarian dishes. The coconut bacon in this book gets its boldness from this ingredient.

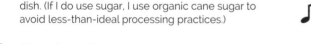
Last but not least:

Good music Music is crucial to how my meals turn out. I have to set the mood when I start creating. Music has always been my outlet for healing so adding good tunes to the mix while cooking seems natural to me.

Brunch & Breakfast

Masa Cakes Benedict with Smoked Tofu, Refried Black Beans & Chimichurri Rojo

4–6 SERVINGS

 Check ingredients if buying ready-made smoked tofu

This is a fun brunch item that takes traditional eggs Benedict to another level. The sweet corn cake, the smokiness of tofu, the creaminess of refried beans, and the tangy chimichurri all balance each other— there are definitely no boring flavors here! While preparing this dish requires several steps, it's fairly easy to execute and absolutely worth adding to your morning brunch staples.

MASA CAKES

- 1 cup sweet corn (frozen or fresh)
- 1 stick or ½ cup cold vegan butter
- 2 cups masa harina (or maize flour/corn meal if you can't find masa harina)
- 1 tablespoon agave
- 1 cup warm water or vegetable stock

SMOKED TOFU

- 1 pack smoked tofu. If you can't find smoked tofu, use pre-baked tofu
- Oil, for sautéing

REFRIED BLACK BEANS

- 1 can black beans, reserve the liquid
- ½ teaspoon ground cumin

CHIMICHURRI ROJO

- 1 cup finely diced roasted red pepper (capsicum)
- 1 tablespoon fresh parsley, chopped small
- 1 tablespoon finely chopped fresh cilantro (coriander)
- ½ teaspoon smoked paprika
- 2 garlic cloves, smashed and minced
- Pinch of red chili flakes
- ⅛ teaspoon orange zest
- 1 tablespoon olive oil

FOR THE CAKES

1 In a food processor or blender, pulse the sweet corn until it's broken up but not pureed. Alternatively, smash it by hand with a mortar and pestle.

2 In a medium-sized mixing bowl, crumble the butter into the masa with your hands until you have a coarse sand-like consistency. Add the remaining masa cake ingredients.

3 Mix by hand until the dough has formed a ball. It will be slightly sticky. Form six balls from the dough and let them rest for a few minutes. The dough can be delicate so be gentle when handling it.

4 In a greased skillet, sauté the cakes over a medium–high heat in a few tablespoons of oil, flattening the balls slightly with a spatula. Cook on each side for about 2–3 minutes or until they are golden brown. Transfer to a paper towel-lined plate. You may place them in a preheated oven at around 200°F (100°C) to keep warm.

FOR THE SMOKED TOFU*

1 Drain and pat the tofu dry with a paper towel. Cut the tofu lengthwise into thirds and then cut in half. You should have six pieces.

2 Heat 1 tablespoon of oil in a medium-sized sauté pan. Sear the tofu in the pan with a little salt and pepper until it's golden brown on both sides, which will take about 2–3 minutes per side.

* If you're using regular (unsmoked) baked tofu, add a few dashes of liquid smoke to the pan while sautéing. Just before turning off the heat, add ½ tablespoon of maple syrup or agave.

FOR THE REFRIED BLACK BEANS

1 Heat the beans in a skillet with their liquid on a high heat, for about 4–5 minutes. Add salt and a little cumin to taste.

2 Transfer to a blender and blend until just pureed.

FOR THE CHIMICHURRI ROJO

1 Put the peppers, parsley, cilantro and garlic on a chopping board and roughly chop together.

2 Add the spices, juice, oil, and salt. Mix together in a small bowl.

SERVE

Plate the masa cakes. Spoon over the refried black beans and top with the tofu and chimichurri.

Sweet Risotto with Plantains & Orange Amaretto Sauce

4–6 SERVINGS

This recipe is one of my favorites in this book. It was developed while I was jamming in the van one day. It's also a bit nostalgic. I grew up eating rice pudding, which my grandmother made with cinnamon and raisins. I have added plantains, orange, and amaretto to honor Puerto Rican flavors but also simply because I had these ingredients on hand in my van that day and was feeling inspired.

Enjoy this dish hot or cold (I prefer it at room temperature), as a breakfast, dessert, or a snack when you need a comforting, stick-to-your-ribs bowl of goodness. If you can't find plantains you could use yellow, ripe bananas, but the dish will taste different.

RICE

½ cup arborio rice

2 cans full-fat coconut milk

1 tablespoon agave or your favorite sweetener

SAUCE

1 tablespoon butter

1 large ripe yellow plantain, sliced into 1-inch (2.5 cm) slices

Pinch of cinnamon

1 tablespoon amaretto liqueur

Zest and juice of 1 orange (keep separate)

¼ teaspoon almond extract

Pinch of salt

½ cup plant-based milk

½ cup sweetened coconut condensed milk

DIRECTIONS

1 Add the rice and coconut milk to a medium-sized pot. Simmer, covered, for 20–25 minutes over a medium heat, stirring occasionally. You may need to add a bit of water toward the end if the liquid has absorbed before the cooking time is up.

2 Meanwhile, heat the butter in a medium-sized sauté pan over medium–high heat. Add the plantains and cinnamon and cook for 2–3 minutes on each side.

3 Add the amaretto. Once it reduces by half, add the orange juice, almond extract, a pinch of salt, and plant-based milk.

4 Simmer until the milk starts to thicken, approximately 3–4 minutes, and then stir in the coconut condensed milk. Heat for another few minutes and then cut the heat.

SERVE

Serve the risotto in a bowl, topping with the sauce and plaintains. Sprinkle with orange zest.

"It took me years to find my voice and to truly acknowledge my yearning for an alternative lifestyle. Once I dove into the unknown, I found it to be a safe haven."

Guava-Stuffed French Toast with Coconut Syrup

4–6 SERVINGS

This dish was one of the first things I ever made for my friends in college. I stuffed some bread with cream cheese and jam and rolled it in cornflakes. I don't believe my friends ever forgot this, so it felt right to resurrect it here as an ode to where my creativity started. I've given it a little bit of an upgrade with the coconut syrup, inspired by one that I tasted that was imported from Hawaii—a flavor that has stuck with me for many years.

If you can't find guava jam, feel free to use whatever preserve you enjoy most. I recommend a thicker bread that is at least a day old. This will ensure it doesn't become soggy when it absorbs the milk mixture.

TOAST

- 1 chia egg (1 tablespoon chia seeds to 3 tablespoons water)
- 1 cup unsweetened plant-based milk (I use soy)
- 1 teaspoon almond extract
- 2 tablespoons agave
- 1 teaspoon ground cinnamon
- 2 tablespoons butter, melted
- 4 slices day-old challah or vegan brioche, 1 inch (2.5 cm) thick
- 2 cups granola

GUAVA CREAM CHEESE

- ½ cup guava jam or paste
- ½ cup cream cheese

COCONUT SYRUP

- 1 cup full-fat coconut milk
- 1–2 tablespoons agave
- 1 teaspoon cornstarch slurry (1 teaspoon cornstarch mixed with 1 teaspoon water)

DIRECTIONS

1 First, make the chia egg by mixing the water and chia together and letting it sit for 5 minutes to thicken.

2 In a mixing bowl, mix the plant-based milk, almond extract, agave, cinnamon, chia egg, and 1 tablespoon of melted butter.

3 Mix the guava jam and cream cheese together in a bowl.

4 Make a slit, lengthwise, into the sides of one side of the bread. Fill the slits with the cream cheese mixture using a spoon or pastry bag.

5 In a small pot, heat the coconut milk and agave over a medium heat until it starts to simmer. Add the cornstarch slurry and stir until the mixture thickens, about 1 minute. Set aside to cool.

6 Add the granola to a baking tray or large plate to toss the bread into it.

7 Heat a large skillet or griddle over a medium heat and add the remaining butter.

8 In stages, dip the stuffed toast into the milk mixture and then into the granola.

9 Add the toast to the skillet or griddle in batches and cook for about 3–4 minutes per side. Make sure it is nice and browned.

SERVE

Serve with the coconut syrup.

Stewed Banana Oatmeal

4–6 SERVINGS

This recipe is dedicated to my friend François. My wife and I were camping on the beach in Cabo Pulmo, Baja Mexico, when this man pulled up in his truck camper. We were immediately annoyed because we'd had the whole beach to ourselves before his arrival. After about an hour he approached us, introducing himself and telling us that he'd been coming to this spot every year for ten years. He was planning to stay for over a month this time and offered us his canoe, bikes, and company.

We enjoyed a week with him and during that time, he noticed us eating oatmeal from a packet one morning. He was beside himself and told us it was silly to purchase oatmeal when we could make our own. He whipped up this dish and we were hooked. The banana melts into the hot oats and the coconut milk adds richness. It was our go-to breakfast during our time there and we will never forget the friendship of François, who we may never see again.

½ cup oats

1 teaspoon ground cinnamon

1½ cups full-fat coconut milk

1 ripe banana, peeled and mashed

1 tablespoon agave

Handful of toasted walnuts or pecans (optional)

DIRECTIONS

1 In a small pot, combine all the ingredients over a medium heat.

2 Allow to simmer for 10–15 minutes, covered, stirring occasionally, until it's creamy and soft.

SERVE

Serve topped with toasted walnuts or pecans (optional).

"The banana melts into the hot oats and the coconut milk adds richness."

Loaded Potato Pancakes

4–6 SERVINGS

Potato pancakes are such a fun way to add to a brunch spread especially when you roll all the flavors of brunch into one pancake, as I've done here. If you are a fan of sweet and savory brunch food and dare to be adventurous, these would be great topped with a sweet fruit compote or syrup, too.

1 flax egg (½ tablespoon flax seeds mixed with 1½ tablespoons plant-based milk)

2 russet potatoes, peeled and grated

½ sweet onion, grated

2 small sweet peppers (capsicums), diced small

1 soysage link, diced small

2 garlic cloves, minced

¼ cup all-purpose (plain) flour

¼ teaspoon smoked paprika

1 tablespoon nootch (nutritional yeast)

Reserved potato starch (see instructions)

1 scallion (spring onion), chopped small

Pinch of salt

DIRECTIONS

1 Mix the flax egg (or another favorite egg substitute) and let it sit for 5 minutes to thicken.

2 Grate the peeled potatoes and onion together using the large blade of a box grater or the grater attachment on a mixer.

3 Place the potato and onion mixture in a cheesecloth or kitchen towel and squeeze out the excess liquid. Do not discard the liquid! Reserve it and set it aside.

4 In a small sauté pan, sauté the peppers, soysage, and garlic together with a little oil over a medium–high heat, for 3–4 minutes, or until browned. Set aside.

5 To a clean bowl, add the strained and grated potato and onion mixture, flour, flax egg, paprika, nootch, sautéed sweet peppers, and soysage.

6 Carefully pour out the water from the reserved potato liquid. The starch will remain on the bottom of the bowl. Add this to the potato mixture and mix well. The mixture will be slightly sticky. If it is too wet, add a bit more flour. If it is too dry, add a bit of plant-based milk.

7 Add about ¼ inch (½ cm) of oil to a frying pan.

8 Using an ice cream scoop, scoop the batter and place in the preheated oil. Flatten with a spatula.

9 Cook in batches, about three or four pancakes at a time, for 2–3 minutes per side, or until golden brown.

10 Remove from the pan with a slotted spatula or spoon and place on a sheet tray lined with a paper towel.

SERVE

Season immediately and add the chopped scallion and any other favorite toppings with a good pinch of salt.

RECOMMENDED TOPPINGS

Fresh cilantro (coriander), chopped

Annatto and orange butter (pg 155)

Charred scallion aioli (pg 144)

Sour cream and cheese

"My spirit was longing for a change.
I still loved to cook but the idea of seeing
the world became more persistent."

Chilaquiles: Tortillas in a Chili Simmering Sauce

4–6 SERVINGS

 When made with 100% corn tortilla chips

This is a go-to comfort meal of mine that is easy to whip up. Who doesn't enjoy tortilla chips smothered with a richly flavored sauce? If you haven't had the pleasure of overindulging in this traditional Mexican staple, now is your chance. Feel free to add as many additional toppings as you like. The chilis tend to lend the sauce bitterness, so if you prefer a sweeter sauce, add more agave for balance. You may also consider substituting the pasilla and guajillo chilis here for your favorite dried chilis, which provide a medium spice level.

Tortilla chips

SAUCE

4 Roma tomatoes, roughly chopped

¼ yellow onion, roughly chopped

4 garlic cloves, smashed

¼ cup oil

2 dried guajillo chilies, deseeded and destemmed

2 dried pasilla chilies, deseeded and destemmed

Vegetable stock (if needed)

1 teaspoon oregano

1 tablespoon agave

Juice of 1 orange

TOPPINGS

Fresh cilantro (coriander)

Thinly sliced radish

Onion, diced small

DIRECTIONS

1 Place tomatoes, onion, and garlic on a sheet tray and broil in the oven on high for about 5 minutes or until slightly charred. Turn them halfway through. Alternatively, you can toast these items in a sauté pan over a medium heat for 5 minutes, or until slightly charred.

2 To a frying pan, add the oil and heat the chilis over a medium heat for a few minutes until fragrant and dark red. Make sure to turn them as they can burn easily. When the chilis are done, reserve the oil.

3 In a high-powered blender, blend the chilis and the remaining ingredients, including the reserved chili oil, until well blended. Add salt to taste. (The sauce will be slightly thick so add vegetable stock to thin out if necessary).

4 Place the sauce in a pot and simmer over a low heat for 8–10 minutes. Stir frequently so it doesn't burn.

SERVE

Arrange tortilla chips on a platter. Pour sauce over the chips and top with your favorite toppings. Drizzle with Queso (pg 136) or Poblano Aioli (pg 143).

Handhelds, Salads & Soups

Tempura-Fried Squash Tacos with Sweet Corn Crema, Tamarind BBQ Sauce & Orange Sesame Slaw

4–6 SERVINGS

This recipe is one of those creations that happened spontaneously on a day when I was supposed to be focused on something else. Yet, really good music led to random ideas and took me down a completely different path... Behold, one of the most curious recipes I've devised but one that I'd happily eat several times a week. This is definitely an ode to happy accidents.

TEMPURA SQUASH

Vegetable oil, for shallow-frying

1 small acorn squash (winter squash) or butternut squash (butternut pumpkin), cut widthwise into ¼ inch (0.5 cm) slices

Rice flour, for coating

TEMPURA BATTER

1 cup rice flour, plus extra for coating

1 cup sparkling water, chilled

¼ cup favorite egg alternative (pg 10 and 12), chilled

SWEET CORN CREMA

1 cup frozen sweet corn, thawed

1 garlic clove, smashed

1½ cups full-fat coconut milk

¼ teaspoon ground cumin

1 tablespoon agave or maple syrup

TAMARIND BBQ SAUCE

2 fl oz (4 tablespoons) tamarind concentrate

1 tablespoon tamari or liquid aminos

1 tablespoon plum sauce

2 tablespoons ketchup

2 tablespoons sweet chili sauce

Juice of ½ orange

2 dashes of liquid smoke

1 teaspoon sesame oil

1 tablespoon agave

SLAW

½ head of cabbage, thinly sliced

2 scallions (spring onions), thinly sliced

Zest and juice of ½ orange

¼ red onion, thinly sliced

½ tablespoon toasted pepitas

⅓ cup vegan mayo

1 tablespoon agave

1 tablespoon rice-wine vinegar

Dash of liquid smoke

Dash of sesame oil

DIRECTIONS

1 For the squash, peel the skin, cut off the ends, then cut it in half lengthwise, scooping out the seeds, then cut it widthwise into ¼ inch (0.5 cm) slices.

2 To prepare the tempura batter: In a mixing bowl, combine the rice flour, sparkling water, egg alternative, and salt and mix well. Keep chilled until ready for use. Also prepare a plate of rice flour with a little salt and pepper for coating. Set the squash and batter station aside.

3 For the corn crema, add all of the ingredients to a small pot and simmer for 4–5 minutes over a medium heat. Transfer to a blender and blend until smooth and creamy. Adjust the salt if necessary.

4 For the BBQ sauce, add all the ingredients to a small pot and simmer for about 10 minutes over a medium heat, or until slightly thickened.

5 For the slaw, add all the vegetables and pepitas to a large bowl. Combine the remaining ingredients in a separate bowl and mix well. Right before serving, mix all the ingredients together to dress the slaw.

6 Fill a large frying pan with vegetable oil until it reaches about ¼ inch (0.5 cm) up the side of the pan and heat over a medium–high heat. Coat the squash first in rice flour, salt, and pepper, then dip into the tempura batter, letting the excess drip off. Immediately place into the hot oil and cook for 2–3 minutes until golden brown and crispy and the squash is fork-tender. Place on a paper towel-lined plate and add a little salt if needed.

SERVE

To assemble, warm your favorite tortillas and fill with a few pieces of squash, followed by the slaw, BBQ sauce, and sweet corn crema. Your taste buds are about to get silly.

Seitan Philly

1–2 SERVINGS

The cheesesteak is one of my favorite sandwiches, and thanks to living in a time in which mock meats are incredibly advanced, meatless versions of such culinary staples can be enjoyed without sacrificing flavor. I present it here with mushrooms, onions, and, yes, queso. I know in Philly they're competitive about their cheese but I have always appreciated the messy gooeyness of cheese sauce and, to be honest, vegan cheese still has a long way to go before that same melt factor is going to win me over. And by all means, if you prefer cheese slices, you do you.

1 yellow onion, thinly sliced
Olive oil
½ tablespoon agave
8 oz (230 g) cremini mushrooms, sliced
¼ teaspoon garlic powder
Pinch of paprika
Dash of liquid smoke
Dash of marsala wine (optional)
Favorite sub/baguette
2 oz (50 g) shaved seitan (pg 87), warmed
½ red pepper (capsicum), thinly sliced
½ cup Queso (pg 136)

FOR CARAMELIZED ONIONS

1 To a medium saucepan, add 1 tablespoon of olive oil and the onion. Sauté over a medium heat until brown and caramelized, about 10–12 minutes. Stir occasionally. Add salt, pepper, and agave.

FOR CRISPY MUSHROOMS

1 In another saucepan, add 1 tablespoon oil and the sliced mushrooms, along with the garlic powder, salt, pepper, and paprika.

2 Sauté over a medium–high heat for 10–12 minutes. Do not stir until the end! This will help the mushrooms caramelize and get crispy.

3 After 10 minutes, deglaze the pan with a dash of liquid smoke and marsala wine. Once the liquid has reduced, stir the mushrooms and continue to cook until they are starting to crisp up again.

4 Transfer to a paper towel-lined plate to retain the crispiness until serving.

SERVE

Toast your favorite baguette and fill with the warm, shaved seitan. Top with the mushrooms, onions, and red pepper. (I like to keep the red pepper raw for crunch and texture but you can cook it with the onions if you prefer). Slather on the Queso and enjoy.

"Thanks to living in a time in which mock meats are incredibly advanced, meatless versions of such culinary staples can be enjoyed without sacrificing flavor."

Tamarind Guava BBQ Tempeh Sandwiches

1–2 SERVINGS

 With gluten-free bread

I got the idea for this dish while I was experimenting with tempeh to win over a friend who had never had it before. They loved BBQ so I used that as a starting point. The tang of the tamarind in this sauce balances the sweetness of the guava. I used dry spices to enhance the BBQ flavor of the tempeh. The caramelized onions add a nice creamy texture. This sandwich is simple to make and bold in flavor.

Favorite sub or roll

Caramelized onions
(pg 22)

BBQ SAUCE

1 cup ketchup

2 tablespoons guava
paste

1 inch (2.5 cm) piece of
(as in pinch of) ginger,
grated

2 garlic cloves, minced

1 tablespoon agave

1 teaspoon liquid
smoke

Pinch of allspice

Dash of hot sauce
(optional)

¼ cup tamarind paste

Juice of 1 orange

Capful of apple-cider
vinegar

TEMPEH

1 teaspoon olive oil

1 teaspoon paprika

¼ teaspoon onion
powder

Pinch of dried thyme

1 teaspoon garlic
powder

¼ teaspoon mustard
powder

1 tablespoon olive oil

1 8 oz (225 gram)
pack of tempeh,
cut lengthwise and
then in half into
four pieces

FOR THE BBQ SAUCE

1 Add all the ingredients to a medium saucepan and bring to a boil, then reduce to a simmer for about 5–10 minutes. Season with salt and pepper. The sauce should be slightly thick. Allow to cool.

FOR THE TEMPEH

1 Mix all the spices together in a small mixing bowl. Coat the tempeh pieces in the spice mixture so both sides are covered.

2 In a large skillet, add the olive oil to coat the pan. Add the tempeh and cook over a medium–high heat for 3–4 minutes per side.

3 Make the caramelized onions as per the Seitan recipe on pg 22.

SERVE

Slather the tempeh with the BBQ sauce and assemble on the bread with the caramelized onions.

C.B.L.T.: Coconut Bacon, Lettuce & Tomato Sandwich with Aji Amarillo Aioli

1–2 SERVINGS

 Use gluten-free bread to make it gluten free

When I ate meat, bacon was my weakness. Now that I eat a plant-based diet, I recognize that it wasn't the bacon itself that was so appealing: it was the combination of crunchy textures and smoky, savory flavors with cool, crisp lettuce, tomato, and mayo on bread. The combination is magical. This plant-based version takes the classic B.L.T. up a notch with tang from the aioli and a bit of spice. You won't feel weighed down or miss out on flavor with this bacon substitute.

¼ cup Coconut bacon (pg 94)

Favorite bread, toasted if preferred

Butter, for spreading

Lettuce leaves rinsed and shredded

1 tomato, sliced

Aji Amarillo Aioli (pg 143)

DIRECTIONS

1   Prepare the coconut bacon according to the instructions on pg 94.

2   Toast and butter your bread if you'd like.

SERVE

Assemble a sandwich with the coconut bacon, lettuce, tomato, and aioli on your favorite bread.

"For any recipes using plant-based proteins, feel free to replace with actual meat substitutes if you wish."

Superfood Salad with Smoky Tahini Beetroot Vinaigrette

4–6 SERVINGS

This salad takes me back to my time in the Adirondack Mountains of New York. My wife and I spent several days camped at a serene spot in the forest, beside a lake. We had a lovely fire and a hammock strung between the trees. On one fairly hot day we decided a salad was on the menu for lunch. At the time, Abi and I were creating cooking videos for our YouTube channel and I wanted to focus on the flavors of the dressing. We had some beets (beetroot) and the vivid purple color gave me the idea to make the dressing the star of the dish. The rest of the ingredients unfolded from there. Behold, this superfood salad.

This dressing is one of my favorites and is excellent for plant-based foodies who once enjoyed bacon, or who just appreciate a smoky flavor. While it does contain a lot of ingredients, if you don't have all of them on hand, just omit! All of the ingredients can be prepped ahead of time if you're planning a dinner party menu. You can also cook the sweet potatoes and the beets in the same pan, to save time.

- 1 small sweet potato, cooked and diced medium
- 2 cups vegetable stock or water
- ½ cup black rice
- 1–2 pieces broccoletti or 1 small crown of broccoli, including the stems and florets
- 4 oz (115 g) tempeh halved, then cut lengthwise into strips
- 1 tablespoon coconut oil
- ¼ teaspoon ground turmeric
- ⅛ teaspoon paprika
- 1 teaspoon agave
- 3–4 oz (100 g) kale, rinsed and shredded

- ½ bunch parsley, rinsed and roughly chopped
- 1 small avocado, sliced and salted
- ¼ small red onion, thinly sliced
- 1 oz (30 g) red cabbage, thinly sliced
- Handful of fresh blackberries (or other favorite berry), rinsed
- Chia seeds, roasted sesame seeds, cilantro (coriander), or walnuts to garnish (optional)

DRESSING

- 2 small beets (beetroot)
- 1 tablespoon white miso paste
- 2 tablespoons tahini
- zest and juice of 1 small lemon
- 1¼ tablespoons agave
- ½ inch piece ginger, peeled and grated
- A few dashes of liquid smoke
- 2 teaspoons apple-cider vinegar
- 1 tablespoon dijon mustard
- 1 tablespoon avocado or grapeseed oil

DIRECTIONS

1 Preheat your oven to 400°F (200°C).

2 Lightly salt and oil the beets and sweet potatoes and place on a foil-lined sheet pan, making sure to keep them separate (the beets are part of the dressing but the sweet potatoes are not). Roast for 50–60 minutes, or until completely tender. Set the sweet potatoes aside to cool.

FOR THE DRESSING

Peel the skin off the beets in a towel so you don't burn or stain yourself. Roughly chop them and add them to a high-speed blender, along with the remaining dressing ingredients. Blend until smooth. Add a bit of water if the dressing is too thick for your liking.

FOR THE BLACK RICE

Bring 2 cups of water or vegetable stock to the boil. Add the rice. Cover and simmer for 40–45 minutes, or until the liquid has absorbed and the rice is tender. When cooked, the rice will still be somewhat chewy.

FOR THE BROCCOLETTI

Boil florets in a pot of salted water until tender, about 3–4 minutes. Drain.

FOR THE TEMPEH

1 Sauté in a small pan with the coconut oil over a medium–high heat for 2–3 minutes per side.

2 Add a few pinches of turmeric, salt, and paprika.

3 Once browned, turn off the heat and add a drizzle of agave or maple syrup.

SERVE

Arrange the salad ingredients in a salad bowl. Place the dressing in a carafe in the center of the salad bowl for the best effect.

"These recipes are a part of a vivid process of self-discovery that emerged through the destinations that inspired them."

Nat's Ultimate Burritos

4–6 SERVINGS

These babies were invented at a nomad event in the desert, known as Skooliepalooza. We spent ten days among hundreds of nomads, living in school buses, vans, and cars, all coming together to make art and memories. It was a life-changing experience for me and while there, I decided to make burritos for whoever came by. On the first day, I was out of burritos within fifteen minutes and felt I needed to redeem myself because so many people waiting in line had to go without. Two days later, I made ninety burritos and left my mark on that event. Every time I make this recipe, I am reminded of a very transformative moment in my life and one that kickstarted a dramatic shift in my personal growth. I love how the memory of food and music have the ability to do that.

Burrito shells
Queso (pg 136; optional)
Poblano aioli (pg 143)

RICE

1¼ – 1½ cups vegetable stock or water
Juice and zest of 1 orange
1 cup jasmine rice
1 tablespoon butter
1 tablespoon fresh cilantro (coriander), chopped

SALSA

1 fresh pomegranate
¼ bunch of fresh cilantro (coriander), chopped
A squeeze of lime juice
A squeeze of orange juice
½ tablespoon agave
½ shallot, minced
1 jalapeño, deseeded and minced

BRAISED PINTOS

1 tablespoon olive oil
1 small yellow onion, peeled and diced
3-4 garlic cloves, smashed
½ tablespoon tomato paste
¼ cup Sofrito (pg 139)
½ teaspoon garlic powder
1 teaspoon cumin
¼ teaspoon ground coriander
1 cup vegetable stock
2 cans pinto beans, liquid reserved

FOR THE RICE

1 To a medium pot, add the stock or water, orange juice, and some salt, and bring to the boil.

2 Stir in the rice and bring the heat down to a simmer.

3 Cover and cook for about 20 minutes.

4 Fluff and add butter, orange zest, and cilantro.

FOR THE SALSA

1 Cut the ends off of the pomegranate, then cut into quarters. Pop out the seeds into a bowl and discard the white pith.

2 Add the remaining ingredients and toss.

FOR THE BEANS

Place the olive oil in a large pot and sauté the onion, garlic, tomato paste, sofrito, and spices over a medium–high heat for 4–5 minutes, or until the onion is tender. Add the stock and beans and simmer until hot, about another 4–5 minutes. Taste and adjust the salt if necessary.

SERVE

Place all the ingredients in your favorite warmed burrito shell. Roll and enjoy. Add Queso (cheese dip) if you're feeling frisky!

Napa Cabbage & Orange Salad with Chili Pepitas & Creamy Guava Vinaigrette

1–2 SERVINGS

There's a lot to be said for a simple, well-balanced salad. This recipe is undramatic, unlike the superfood salad on page 32. It has just four components, which really complement each other. It's a great dish to make for lunch or as an accompaniment to one of the heavier meals in this book. Enjoy the crunchiness of cabbage, the tangy tartness of orange, the subtle spice of the pepitas, and the sweet creaminess of the dressing.

½ cup pepitas

1 teaspoon maple syrup

½ teaspoon chili powder

Squeeze of fresh lime juice

1 tablespoon guava jam or paste

½ cup mayonnaise

¼ small shallot, peeled and chopped

zest and juice of 1 orange, plus 1 orange, peeled and cut into segments (see Tip)

2 teaspoons white balsamic or rice-wine vinegar

¼ head of Napa cabbage (Chinese cabbage/ wombok), rinsed, cored, and chopped to your desired size. (Can be substituted for a different type of cabbage, radicchio, or whatever else excites you)

Small handful of fresh cilantro (coriander), chopped, to garnish

TIP

To make orange supremes, peel the entire orange down to the flesh. Slice in between the membrane, carefully removing the orange segment. Repeat between each section of membrane. This gives you clean segments of pure orange delight!

FOR PEPITAS

1 Preheat the oven to 360°F (180°C).

2 Combine the pepitas, maple syrup, chili powder, and lime in a mixing bowl and stir until evenly mixed.

3 Spread on a parchment paper-lined baking sheet and bake for around 5 minutes, until lightly browned, turning once. Remove from the oven and sprinkle with a little salt.

FOR GUAVA VINAIGRETTE

1 In a small bowl, mix together the guava jam, mayonnaise, shallots, orange juice and zest, and vinegar until smooth.

SERVE

Arrange the cabbage, orange segments, and pepitas in a bowl. Drizzle with the vinaigrette and enjoy.

Grilled Romaine Lettuce, Charred Tomato, Green Chili Croutons & Manchego Dressing

2–4 SERVINGS

 Omit croutons to make this gluten free

A grilled salad is a game changer: the char and flame broil from the grill gives the ingredients more flavor, which definitely keeps the salad from being boring. This is a hit among my camp friends and is a great salad for people who don't like salads (or, who don't *think* they like salads!) because it doesn't really taste like a salad. Add Coconut bacon (pg 94) or shredded Seitan (pg 87) to make this a complete meal, or serve as a side or a starter course.

SALAD

2 heads romaine (cos) lettuce, rinsed and cut lengthwise (to give four halves)

3 tablespoons olive oil

½ pound (225 g) cherry tomatoes

CROUTONS

¼ cup olive oil

1 tablespoon canned green chilis, drained

2–3 garlic cloves, minced

½ cup day-old bread cut into cubes (I recommend sourdough)

DRESSING

½ cup Manchego cheese, shredded (you can replace with vegan cheese)

½ cup mayonnaise

¼ cup buttermilk (or replace with vegan plant-based milk plus 1 tablespoon lemon juice)

Juice of ½ lemon

FOR THE GRILLED ROMAINE (COS) LETTUCE

On a clean grill or griddle, place the oiled romaine halves face down and gently press into the grate. Cook for 2–3 minutes and flip for another 2 minutes. You should have a nice char on each side.

FOR THE TOMATOES

1 Toss the tomatoes with a little oil, salt, and pepper.

2 Cook on the stove in a hot cast-iron pan, until softened and charred. Alternatively, place the tomatoes on a sheet pan and broil in the oven at 500°F (260°C) for 4–5 minutes, or until charred.

FOR THE CROUTONS

1 Mix the oil, green chilis, and garlic in a bowl. Toss in cubes of bread and mix until coated.

2 Place on a baking sheet and bake in the oven at 400°F (205°C) for 10–12 minutes, stirring once halfway. The croutons should be golden brown. Let them cool.

FOR THE DRESSING

Blend all the ingredients in a blender or food processor.

SERVE

Assemble each lettuce half on a dish, drizzle with the dressing, and top with the croutons and tomatoes. I also suggest a squeeze of fresh lemon to finish.

Chanterelle & Hazelnut Ramen

6–8 SERVINGS

This dish will always mean a lot to me. Not only am I in love with its rich flavors, but it takes me to a particular memory that I will never forget, when I was visiting a friend in Philly. We decided to collaborate on a dinner together one night, and walked to a local farmer's market to pick up some chanterelle mushrooms. Our friend made a stellar cocktail (a whiskey cocktail with grapefruit, blood orange soda, and rosemary simple syrup, in case you're interested!) and set the table in true interior-designer fashion. I made the ramen and we filmed the experience for our YouTube channel.

Most of our videos were set up as how-to guides, but this was more like poetry. We put on music and just started creating. Abi filmed the process and the outcome was an organic flow of motion art, food, and passions intertwined. Every time I make this meal, I smile and get goosebumps at the memory. I consider most of my food to be humble, but this dish is sexy, elevated, and one to share with friends.

1 bulb of garlic

3–4 tablespoons olive oil

3–4 sprigs of fresh rosemary

1 cup whole hazelnuts

1 inch (2.5 cm) knob of ginger, mashed, smashed (skin on is fine)

1 medium yellow onion, halved and studded with 3 whole cloves

12 oz (350 g) fresh chanterelle mushrooms (alternatively, 3 oz/85 g dried chanterelles)

1 tablespoon tomato paste

1 tablespoon red miso paste

½ tablespoon plum sauce or jam

A few dashes of liquid smoke

About 3 quarts (3 liters) vegetable stock

2 sheets of dried kombu (edible kelp)

2 ears of corn, shucked (save the cobs)

16 oz (450 g) packet of your favorite ramen noodles

DIRECTIONS

1 Preheat the oven to 400°F (200°C). Coat the bulb of garlic with olive oil and roast with one sprig of rosemary in aluminum foil for about 30 minutes, or until completely tender.

2 Meanwhile, toast the hazelnuts in a dry sauté pan over a medium–high heat until fragrant and browned, about 4–5 minutes. Place them in a food processor and set aside—do not blend yet.

3 Cut the roasted garlic bulb open to release the fragrance and add to a large heavy bottomed pot along with the rosemary and reserved oil from the baking process. Add a couple more swigs of olive oil to the pan.

4 Add the smashed ginger and the chanterelles. Sauté for a few minutes over a medium–high heat (or until the dried mushrooms have reconstituted).

5 Add the halved onion to the pot, skin-side up. Sauté until the onion is charred almost black.

6 Remove the chanterelles and set aside.

7 Add the tomato paste, miso paste, and plum sauce. Stir and let the ingredients toast over a medium–high heat for a few minutes.

8 Deglaze the pan with the liquid smoke, then add the vegetable stock and kombu. Throw in the shucked corn cobs.

9 In a separate small pan, sauté the corn kernels over a high heat until they start to pop and caramelize. Turn off the heat and set them aside.

10 Take the remaining rosemary sprigs, set them on fire (make sure they are smoking!) and throw them into the pot. Immediately cover the pot to keep the rosemary smoke in and simmer over a low heat for about 1–1½ hours, until the ramen broth has reduced by about one quarter.

11 Ladle a bit of broth into the food processor and blend the hazelnuts. Strain this hazelnut puree through a cheesecloth and into the broth. (Straining is important to achieve a smooth consistency).

12 Continue cooking the broth for another 20 minutes. Cut the heat and strain the broth in a colander.

13 Add the chanterelles back to the pot, alongside the reserved corn kernels.

14 Cook the noodles according to the instructions on the packet.

SERVE

Add the broth and noodles to a bowl, along with your favorite toppings.

"I consider most of my food to be humble, but this dish is sexy, elevated, and one to share with friends."

Coconut Soup with Pistachio Pesto

2–4 SERVINGS

This is another recipe that came about when my wife and I were creating pop-up oceanside restaurant menus in Mexico. We constructed a nice firepit and seating area outside our campers and built the menus each week based on fusion cuisine centered around Mexican food. This was part of our Indian-Mexican fusion menu. I wanted a light and delicate but flavorsome soup to start the multi-course meal. The coconut milk is subtle and the pesto gives the soup a slight brightness. I love this dish. It's simple and, sometimes, that's the best move.

I recommend toasting some naan bread or pita to dip into the soup. Note that, because of the simplicity of this soup, it's important to get the salt/sweet balance absolutely right. Salt a little, add some agave, and taste. If it isn't to your liking, add a bit more salt or agave. I always season in stages.

SOUP

3 garlic cloves, minced

1¼ inch (3 cm) knob of fresh ginger, grated

1 tablespoon butter

2 cans full-fat coconut milk★

¼ teaspoon ground cardamom

1 serrano or jalapeño pepper, roasted, deseeded, and minced (optional but recommended)

1–2 tablespoons agave

PESTO

⅓ cup shelled pistachios plus extra chopped pistachios, to garnish

2–3 garlic cloves, roughly chopped

3 cups fresh basil

¼ cup green olives

½ cup extra-virgin olive oil

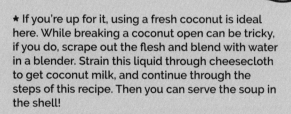

★ If you're up for it, using a fresh coconut is ideal here. While breaking a coconut open can be tricky, if you do, scrape out the flesh and blend with water in a blender. Strain this liquid through cheesecloth to get coconut milk, and continue through the steps of this recipe. Then you can serve the soup in the shell!

DIRECTIONS

1 Sauté the garlic and ginger with the butter in a medium pot. Cook over a medium heat until the garlic and ginger are fragrant and becoming tender.

2 Add the coconut milk and cardamom and season with salt and pepper. Simmer, covered, for about 10 minutes. Toss in the roasted chili pepper of your choice, along with the agave.

3 For the pesto, pulse all the ingredients (except the oil) in a food processor or blender. (If using a blender, add half the oil to get it started.) Blend for 1 minute.

4 Switch the food processor/blender to low and slowly drizzle in the oil until combined. Taste for salt.

SERVE

Serve the soup topped with pesto and some extra chopped pistachios.

"This lifestyle was kind of a foreign concept
to people working normal jobs and living
the typical 'American dream.'
I had always been one to go against the grain,
never really fitting in and always interested
in less mainstream pursuits."

Peanut Stew with Sweet Potato, Peppers & Coconut Milk

6–8 SERVINGS

This hearty, robust dish is inspired by a West African peanut stew. I use sweet potatoes, which pair well with peanut butter and coconut milk, creating a rich and creamy broth with a touch of sweetness. I spent most of my culinary career in Charleston, South Carolina, where the cuisine has heavy Caribbean and African influences. A lot of my cooking style is derived from my time there and this dish is a reminder of the place I once called home.

1–2 tablespoons peanut or vegetable oil

1 red bell pepper (capsicum), diced medium

1 small yellow onion, diced medium

1 medium red sweet potato, peeled and cut into ½ inch (1.25 cm) cubes

1½ inch (4 cm) knob of ginger, grated

3–4 garlic cloves, smashed

1 bay leaf

½ tablespoon tomato paste

¼ cup peanut butter

½ teaspoon crushed chili flakes

1 teaspoon ground cumin

1 teaspoon ground coriander

¼ teaspoon dried thyme

2 teaspoons tamari or liquid aminos

2–3 cups vegetable stock

1 can full-fat coconut milk

1 tablespoon maple syrup

½ cup roasted peanuts, chopped

1 tablespoon cilantro (coriander)

DIRECTIONS

1 In a large pot, heat the oil. Add the pepper, onion, and sweet potato and sauté over a medium–high heat for about 5 minutes.

2 Add the ginger, garlic, bay leaf, tomato paste, peanut butter, and spices and sauté for another 3–4 minutes.

3 Deglaze with the tamari or liquid aminos and then add the vegetable stock.

4 Cover and simmer for 10–15 minutes, or until the potatoes are tender.

5 Add the coconut milk and maple syrup and stir.

6 Check the salt and adjust if necessary.

SERVE

Serve in bowls and top with the roasted peanuts and cilantro if you'd like. Enjoy on its own, over rice, or with a big piece of crusty bread.

Appetizers

Coconut Fry Bread

4–6 SERVINGS

These fried pockets of goodness are great for any occasion. They are tasty as a snack or when accompanying a main meal. I love to have them alongside rice and beans, a salad, or with a stew. They are light and airy and the slight hint of coconut makes them one of my favorite foods. You can enjoy them savory or sweet.

1 cup all-purpose (plain) flour plus extra for dusting
½ teaspoon baking powder
2 teaspoons sugar
½ cup canned full-fat coconut milk
vegetable oil, for shallow-frying

DIRECTIONS

1   In a medium mixing bowl, mix the dry ingredients together.

2   Add the coconut milk and combine to form a ball. Knead for about 2 minutes, then place a damp towel over the bowl and let it rest for 30 minutes.

3   On a lightly floured surface, roll the dough out until it's about ¼ inch (0.5 cm) thick. Cut the dough using a round cookie cutter, or a cup that you have on hand.

4   Add vegetable oil to a deep sauté pan or cast-iron skillet. The oil should come about ¼ inch (0.5 cm) up the side of the pan. If you have a thermometer, keep the oil at 350°F (175°C). If not, keep the oil over a high heat and just pay closer attention to the fry bread as it cooks. Alternatively, you can prepare a deep-fryer at 350°F (175°C).

5   Once the oil is hot, drop the dough circles into the pan in batches, making sure not to overcrowd the pan. Fry on each side for 2–3 minutes, or until golden brown. The dough circles should puff up during the frying process.

SERVE

After removing the fry breads from the pan, place on a paper towel-lined plate. Add a pinch of salt while they are still hot. You can also drizzle agave on them if you'd prefer them sweeter. Serve with Caramelized Scallion Butter (pg 150) and/or Annatto and Orange Butter (pg 155).

"This is the first time I've written recipes down as I've always followed my grandmother's style and allowed intuition to drive my art."

Baked Cabbage Rolls with Picadillo & Aji Amarillo Corn Crema

4–6 SERVINGS

I have always enjoyed elevated comfort food. When I started eating vegan and traveled west, I was introduced to so many plant-based foods that were packed with flavor. I tried spin-offs of classic dishes I had eaten growing up, but with interesting twists. This exploration of unique flavors kick-started my desire to cook plant-based foods that would wow meat lovers. This dish takes cabbage and Picadillo, a Puerto Rican "meat" stew, and creates a new genre of fusion cuisine.

FOR CABBAGE

1 medium head of savoy cabbage

Picadillo "Beefy" Stew (pg 97)

Sweet corn crema (pg 20), made with ½ cup Aji Amarillo Paste (pg 143)

DIRECTIONS

1 Bring a large pot of salted water to the boil.

2 Boil the whole head of cabbage for 3–4 minutes, or just until tender.

3 Remove, drain, and cut the end of the stem off. Carefully remove eight of the largest leaves (approximately the same size). Set aside.

4 Prepare the Picadillo "Beefy" Stew (pg 97) as instructed.

5 Preheat the oven to 375°F (190°C)

6 Lay out the cabbage leaves on a clean surface.

7 Scoop ¼–⅓ cup of the picadillo filling into each cabbage leaf. Start to roll it, tucking both ends inward, and then continue to roll it up completely. Place the roll seam-side down onto a greased baking pan.

8 Continue this process with the rest of the rolls.

9 Top with the remaining filling and the sweet corn crema.

10 Cover with aluminum foil and bake for about 30 minutes. After 30 minutes, uncover and bake for a further 15 minutes. The cabbage will start to get golden brown at the edges and the sauce will be bubbly.

SERVE

Serve the cabbage rolls with a salad or some roasted potatoes.

"Food is a gateway to community and a way to open a conversation."

Empanetzels with Soyrizo & Sweet Plantain

MAKES 8 EMPANETZELS

This recipe is one of my favorites because my wife and I created it together. We took her original pretzel recipe and gave it a makeover. Empanadas are one of my favorite things to eat so we thought it would be awesome to merge the two recipes together and boom! The birth of the empanetzel: basically, a stuffed pretzel hot pocket. I think "empanetzel" deserves its own entry in the dictionary.

0.25 oz (7 g) active dry yeast
1 teaspoon sugar
1 cup warm water (105–110°F/ 40–43°C) or warm light beer
4 cups all-purpose (plain) flour
2 teaspoons salt
Soyrizo (pg 84)
1 ripe yellow plantain, smashed
3 tablespoons melted butter

DIPPING SOLUTION

⅓ cup baking soda (bicarbonate of soda)
6 cups water

DIRECTIONS

1 Preheat oven to 425°F (220°C).

2 Add yeast, sugar, and warm water or beer to a bowl and mix. Cover with a towel and set aside for 10 minutes. It should become foamy.

3 To a separate bowl, add the flour and salt. Create a well in the middle and pour in the yeast mixture and melted butter. Stir to combine and then use your hands to knead into a smooth dough. You may need to add a touch more water.

4 Coat the mixing bowl with a thin layer of oil. Return the dough to the bowl and cover with a towel. Let the dough rise in a warm spot for an hour, or until it has doubled in size.

5 Divide the dough into eight balls. Using a rolling pin, roll each dough ball out until it's about 6 inches (15 cm) in diameter.

6 Fill each round with about ¼ cup of soyrizo filling and some sweet plantain.

7 Fold the dough over, creating a half-moon shape. Pinch the edges together with a fork, making sure it's securely sealed or it will fall apart in the dipping solution.

8 In a medium pot, mix the baking soda and water. Bring it to a boil and then cut the heat.

9 One by one, submerge each empanetzel in the solution with a slotted spoon for just a few seconds each. Immediately transfer to a sheet tray and brush with melted butter.

10 Once they are all out of the solution, bake in the oven for 13–15 minutes, until golden brown.

SERVE

Immediately sprinkle with salt and serve warm.

Guacamole with Caramelized Ginger & Orange

4–6 SERVINGS

Eating and preparing this reminds me of Baja Mexico because this recipe was born on the beach at one of our pop-up dinners. Creating this was a happy accident and I don't believe I can eat regular guacamole anymore. Most people who have tried this say the same thing. It's definitely one of my signature creations and quite a crowd pleaser.

1–2 teaspoons olive oil

1 teaspoon fresh grated ginger

1 garlic clove, smashed into a paste

2 ripe avocados

Juice of 1 orange and ¼ teaspoon zest

1 tablespoon fresh cilantro (coriander), finely chopped

½ tablespoon agave

DIRECTIONS

1 Add the oil to a small saucepan and set over a medium heat.

2 Add the ginger and garlic to the pan and let it caramelize for about 5 minutes, or until the ginger is toasty brown and the garlic is fragrant.

3 Meanwhile, scoop the avocado flesh into a bowl and smash with the zest of the orange, cilantro, and a pinch of salt.

4 Add the orange juice and the agave to the pan and let it reduce by about one quarter, about 3 minutes.

5 Add the ginger mixture to the avocado and mix well.

SERVE

Serve with tortilla chips, fry bread, or throw it onto a rice bowl.

Roasted Strawberry Bruschetta with Pesto Butter & Strawberry Balsamic Glaze

4–6 SERVINGS

 Can be gluten free when made with gluten-free bread

Strawberries and balsamic vinegar were absolutely meant to make love. I would put this bombshell on any menu, for any occasion. It's a great appetizer or accompaniment to any Mediterranean or Italian-themed meal, and I suggest pairing it with wine. All the wine, and conversation.

BRUSCHETTA

1½ cups strawberries, rinsed, hulled

½ cup finely diced tomato

1 tablespoon fresh basil, thinly sliced

PESTO BUTTER

2 cups basil leaves

¼ cup green olives

1–2 large garlic cloves, smashed

1 tablespoon lemon juice

⅓ cup toasted pine nuts

½ tablespoon nootch (nutritional yeast) or vegan parmesan

2 fl oz (4 tablespoons) butter, at room temperature

¼–⅓ cup olive oil

STRAWBERRY BALSAMIC GLAZE

1 cup balsamic vinegar

½ cup diced strawberries

2 tablespoons agave

Pinch each of salt and black pepper

Handful of chopped basil

FOR BRUSCHETTA

1 Preheat your oven to 400°F (200°C).

2 Place the strawberries on a lined sheet tray and roast them whole for 10 minutes. Let them cool slightly and dice small.

3 Toss in a mixing bowl with the tomato and basil. Keep in the fridge until ready to use.

FOR PESTO BUTTER

1 Place all the ingredients, except the olive oil and butter, in a food processor or blender. Run on low and slowly drizzle the oil in. Blend until all the ingredients are incorporated, about 30 seconds.

2 Combine the butter with 2 tablespoons of pesto. Place in the fridge to let it firm up, until ready to use. (The pesto butter and pesto can be kept in the refrigerator for up to 2 weeks.)

FOR GLAZE

1 In a small saucepan, combine all the ingredients and simmer over a low heat until reduced by half, approximately 10–12 minutes. It should just coat a spoon.

2 Blend in a blender on a high-speed setting until smooth, then let it cool. Make sure not to over-cook the glaze as it will turn into a tacky burnt mess. It will continue to thicken as it cools. (You'll want to have your door open or a fan on as the vinegar hits the nose quite hard.)

SERVE

Once all the ingredients are chilled, toast your favorite baguette, spread pesto butter on each piece, top with bruschetta, and drizzle with glaze. Sprinkle with some chopped basil. I put the glaze in a squeeze bottle for easy storage and use.

Main Staples

Creamy Ramen Noodles

1 SERVING

If you love ramen, you have to give this version a try. I took a broth-less ramen and replaced it with this velvety sauce made with coconut milk and tahini. This is now a staple dish in my kitchen.

3 oz (85g) pack of favorite ramen noodles

¼ cup reserved noodle water

1 garlic clove, smashed

¼ teaspoon grated ginger

1 small sweet pepper (capsicum), deseeded and sliced

1 teaspoon sesame oil

1 cup full-fat coconut milk

½ tablespoon fresh orange juice

1 teaspoon porcini or umami powder (optional)

1 teaspoon hoisin sauce

½ tablespoon tahini

1 tablespoon soy sauce

1 tablespoon agave

GARNISH SUGGESTIONS

Fresh cilantro (coriander), chopped

Black sesame seeds

Lime wedges

DIRECTIONS

1 Cook ramen according to the packet. Drain, reserve ¼ cup of cooking liquid, and set noodles aside. Drizzle a bit of oil on the noodles so they don't clump together.

2 In a medium saucepan, sauté the garlic, ginger, and pepper in the sesame oil over a medium heat until tender and fragrant. Don't cook over a high heat as the sesame oil will burn and take on a bitter flavor.

3 Add the remaining ingredients and simmer for about 5 minutes, letting the sauce thicken slighlly.

SERVE

Place the ramen noodles in a big bowl, followed by the sauce. Add your favorite garnishes.

"This exploration of unique flavors kick-started my desire to cook plant-based foods that would wow meat lovers."

Plantain Gnocchi with Meat-Free Mushroom Carnitas

4–6 SERVINGS

I've always loved the combination of savory and sweet, so playing with a dish that is normally savory and flipping it was fun. You have the sweetness of the gnocchi with a rich "meaty" broth. This one is definitely not your typical flavor experience but that's what I'm going for. I grew up with plantains as a staple kitchen item, but for those who did not, it can be an acquired taste. Not a fan? Make sweet potato gnocchi instead. You still get the sweet and savory that will pair well with the "carnitas."

2 ripe yellow plantains (almost black is best)

1 cup all-purpose (plain) flour

¼ teaspoon ground cinnamon

Pinch of ground nutmeg

2 tablespoons water

½ teaspoon brown sugar

Butter, for sautéing

Mushroom carnitas (pg 96)

DIRECTIONS

1 Peel the plantains and cut into 1 inch (2.5 cm) cubes.

2 Prepare a steamer basket or, if you don't have one, bring a pot of water to the boil and place a colander on top. Make sure the water is below the colander and you have a lid on hand.

3 Cover and steam the plantain for about 10 minutes, or until it is completely tender. Let it cool slightly.

4 Transfer the plantains to a mixing bowl and mash them.

5 Add the flour, spices, and sugar and start to fold. Add the water as you fold, just until a ball forms.

6 Now cut the dough in half, rolling each piece out into a 1 inch (2.5 cm) thick rope. Do this by rolling the ball on a clean surface from the middle, outward, with your hands, until it forms a rope.

7 Cut your gnocchi into 1 inch (2.5 cm) pieces.

8 Prepare a pot of boiling salted water. In batches, place the gnocchi gently into the boiling water with a slotted spoon.

9 Let them cook for 3–4 minutes, or until they start to float.

10 Remove them from the water, transfer to a plate, and continue with the remaining dough.

11 From here, sauté the gnocchi in a pan with butter over a medium heat until they start to brown slightly. Make sure they are mostly dry and that your oil is hot so they don't stick.

SERVE

Toss the gnocchi in the carnitas and enjoy!

Smoked Poblano & Manchego Mac 'n' Cheese

6–8 SERVINGS

When I was living in Charleston, South Carolina, before living in a van full time, I did some side gigs outside my regular cooking job. I once did a chef takeover at this super-cute wine and tapas bar downtown, serving a menu of my creation. My menu that night was three different kinds of mac 'n' cheese and I called the menu "macnage *à trois*." Get it? Three dishes. Sexy food. I'll wait here.

Anyways, I ended up selling out and people raved about it for some time after. The experience gave me the idea to sell mac 'n' cheese around town for extra cash. I would create a menu of at least four or five variations of this childhood staple and deliver trays to people. I thoroughly enjoyed getting creative with all the different ways you can put these ingredients together, and it kind of became my little niche for a while. This one is a personal favorite and an ode to my not-so-starving artist days.

16 oz (450 g) macaroni, or your favorite pasta (I like rigatoni)

2 poblano peppers

2 cups half-and-half (low-fat) milk★

2–3 garlic cloves

¼ cup butter

¼ cup all-purpose (plain) flour

1 teaspoon dried mustard powder

⅛ teaspoon paprika

1 cup reserved pasta water

1 bay leaf

10 oz (280 g) Manchego cheese, grated★

1–2 oz (30–55 g) white cheddar, or your favorite cheese, grated★

★ To make this dish vegan, substitute plant-based milk and your favorite vegan cheese.

DIRECTIONS

1 Cook pasta according to the packet in a pot of salted water. Drain, reserving 1 cup pasta water, and drizzle with oil to prevent clumping. Set aside.

2 Broil the poblano peppers in the oven on a sheet tray until mostly blackened. Submerge in water to peel off the skin and remove the seeds and stem. Discard the water.

3 Blend in a high-speed blender with 1 cup of the half-and-half milk and garlic. Add a little salt.

4 To a large saucepan, add the butter, flour, dried mustard and paprika, and stir with a spatula over a medium heat for about 5 minutes. Stir often so the flour doesn't burn.

5 Whisk in the reserved pasta water, remaining milk, and bay leaf. Stir continuously until smooth and creamy.

6 Add salt and simmer until thickened, about 5 minutes.

7 Cut the heat and stir in the cheeses. Toss in the pasta.

SERVE

You can serve as-is or transfer to a baking pan, top with extra cheese, and broil (grill) in the oven until the cheese is bubbly and golden.

Creamy Butternut Squash Pasta, Coconut Bacon & Gingersnap Crumble

6–8 SERVINGS

I thought of this recipe when I was selling holiday sides around my neighborhood. Before taking off on the road, I would make a little extra money each year by making a small menu of sides that people could pick up, ready to go for dinner. I took fall flavors and incorporated them into this creation, but it tastes good at any time of year. Pair this dish with a warm cider by the fire.

½ small butternut squash (butternut pumpkin)

½ teaspoon ground cinnamon

⅛ teaspoon ground nutmeg

¼ teaspoon paprika

1 box favorite pasta (I used bowtie)

2–2½ cups cashew, oat, or soy milk, unsweetened

½ tablespoon nootch (nutritional yeast)

1 tablespoon agave or maple syrup

Coconut bacon (pg 94)

FOR CRUMBLE

10–12 gingersnap cookies

2 large sprigs fresh rosemary, finely chopped

½ teaspoon fresh thyme

2 tablespoons butter, melted

DIRECTIONS

1 Preheat the oven to 375°F (190°C).

2 Lightly oil the squash and add salt, cinnamon, nutmeg, and paprika to the flesh side. Bake on a foil-lined sheet pan, skin-side down, for 35–40 minutes, or until tender.

3 Meanwhile, boil the pasta according to the instructions on the packet. Drain the noodles, drizzle with oil to prevent them from sticking, and set aside. Once the squash has cooled somewhat, peel off the skin and scoop the flesh into a high-speed blender with the plant-based milk, nootch, and agave, until it's smooth. Adjust the salt if necessary.

4 Make the coconut bacon and set aside.

5 In a food processor or blender, pulse the cookies with the rosemary and thyme until crumbly. Mix with the melted butter and toast in a pan for a few minutes, until a light golden brown. Let cool.

6 Put the pasta in a 9 x 13 inch (20 x 30 cm) lightly greased pan and pour the sauce over it, stirring it in well.

7 Top with the cookie crumble mixture.

8 Bake for 15–20 minutes. The crumble should be nice and toasted.

SERVE

Once the pasta is out of the oven, sprinkle with the coconut bacon and prepare for the most sensationally happy mouth.

"I took fall flavors and incorporated them into this creation, but it tastes good at any time of year."

Some Kinda Jumbled Jambalaya

4–6 SERVINGS

I first made this dish for one of our YouTube cooking videos while camping in the Black Hills of South Dakota. A friend had driven all the way from Colorado to spend the weekend with us and we ate this dish before dancing under the stars. I couldn't possibly forget this dish as the memory is just as indulgent. I put a slight spin on this Louisiana classic by adding saffron and annatto, which also makes it a remix of a few different rice dishes from Spain and Puerto Rico. I am a big advocate for everyone coexisting in harmony and I feel the same way about my food.

¼ cup vegetable oil

2 links of your favorite vegan sausage, cut into 1 inch (2.5 cm) chunks

⅛ teaspoon saffron threads

1 red bell pepper (capsicum), diced small

1 small yellow onion, diced small

3–4 garlic cloves, smashed

1 carrot, peeled and diced small

1 celery stalk, diced small

1 jalapeño, deseeded and diced small

1 tablespoon tomato paste

¼ teaspoon annatto powder

1 teaspoon sweet paprika

½ teaspoon crushed chili flakes

1 teaspoon garlic powder

1 teaspoon onion powder

⅛ teaspoon cayenne

¼ teaspoon dried thyme

½ teaspoon dried oregano

2 cups jasmine rice

2½–2¾ cups vegetable stock

1 can stewed tomatoes, chopped and drained

FOR SAUCE

½ cup mayonnaise

2 chipotles in adobo sauce

1 tablespoon agave

Juice of ½ lime

Water to thin

DIRECTIONS

1 In a large saucepan, add 2 tablespoons of the oil to a pan and sauté the sausage chunks over a medium heat until browned on both sides, about 5 minutes. Remove from the pan and set aside.

2 Add a bit more oil and the saffron threads and allow the oil to heat the saffron for a few minutes.

3 Sauté the pepper, onion, garlic, carrot, celery, and jalapeño until tender, about 3–4 minutes.

4 Add the tomato paste and the dried spices and toast for a minute.

5 Mix in the rice and allow to toast for a few minutes.

6 Add the stewed tomatoes and flatten everything down with a spatula until evenly distributed.

7 Add the stock and cover. Simmer for 20–25 minutes, or until the liquid has fully absorbed and the rice is fully cooked. Adjust the salt if necessary.

8 For the sauce, blend all the ingredients in a food processor until smooth.

SERVE

Place in a bowl and drizzle over the sauce.

Coconut Braised Black-Eyed Peas

4–6 SERVINGS

When Covid-19 first hit, my wife and I were just crossing the Mexico border back into the U.S. and hadn't been informed about how bad things had gotten over here. We weren't prepared for what we were about to experience when we arrived, camping for an undetermined amount of time in the forest, far away from anyone. During our time in lockdown, I wanted hearty meals I could cook easily. We had sofrito and black-eyed peas on hand. We served this dish alongside a simple slaw, slow-cooked tomatoes, and fry bread. You could also make this as a filling for a burrito, or eat it with rice. It's a versatile dish, appropriate for endless occasions, and will be a staple for us if the apocalypse ever comes—as well as providing us with some nostalgia of those lockdown times.

½ cup Sofrito (pg 139)
2 cans black-eyed peas, drained and rinsed★
1 cup vegetable stock
1 can full-fat coconut milk
1 tablespoon oil

★ Feel free to use dried beans, just soak them overnight and then cook them in a pressure cooker.

DIRECTIONS

1 Sauté the sofrito in the oil in a medium–large pot over a medium–high heat for a few minutes.

2 Place the beans and vegetable stock in the pot and bring to the boil, then reduce down to a simmer.

3 Cook for 5 minutes to blend with the sofrito and add the coconut milk.

4 Cook for another 3–4 minutes to thicken. Adjust the salt if necessary.

"I am a big advocate for everyone coexisting in harmony and I feel the same way about my food."

Arroz Mamposteao: Puerto Rican Stewed Beans & Rice

4–6 SERVINGS

Rice and beans was a staple in my grandmother's house when I was growing up. White and brown rice were always on hand whenever I wanted a snack. When most of my friends would eat candy or highly processed snack food, I would eat rice and sliced bananas. This recipe is the cream of the crop for me; it's my grandmother through-and-through. I will forever be tied to this food. It represents me more than any other dish in this book and I hope you taste the love and humble goodness that it brings.

1½ cups jasmine rice

1 tablespoon butter

2 tablespoons olive oil

3 garlic cloves, smashed and chopped

1 red pepper (capsicum), diced small

1 small yellow onion, diced small

½ cup Sofrito (pg 139)

1 tablespoon Nikki Mix (pg 152)

1 tablespoon tomato paste

¼ cup stewed canned tomatoes

2 cups vegetable stock

1 can kidney beans or pink beans, drained

¼ cup Manzanilla olives

DIRECTIONS

1 Bring 2 cups of water to the boil in a medium pot. Add the rice with some salt and reduce to a simmer. Cover and cook the rice for 20 minutes. Cut the heat, remove the lid, and fluff the rice. Add the butter and set aside.

2 In a large sauté pan, heat the oil and sauté the garlic, peppers, onion, and sofrito on a medium–high heat for about 5 minutes or until the vegetables have softened.

3 Add the Nikki mix, tomato paste, and canned tomato and sauté for another few minutes.

4 Add the vegetable stock and beans and simmer for a few more minutes. Add the olives.

SERVE

Mix the rice into the beans, or top the rice with the beans if you prefer. You can also top with fresh cilantro (coriander) and serve with Maduros (sweet plantains) (pg 78) if you like.

Braised Kale with Coconut Milk & Tahini

6–8 SERVINGS

This dish was inspired by a chef friend of mine who makes a version with peanut butter instead of tahini. I fell in love with the creaminess and richness the tahini gives the greens, which can sometimes be boring. Now, I find it hard to eat kale any other way. If you're not a fan of this healthy green, let me change your mind. This can be served over creamy polenta, mashed potatoes, rice, or ramen noodles. Or just enjoy it on its own as a hearty bowl of greens.

Coconut oil for sautéing
3–4 garlic cloves, smashed
1 inch (2.5 cm) knob of ginger, grated
½ teaspoon chili flakes
1 lb (450 g) kale, rinsed and chopped small
¼ cup tahini
Dash of apple-cider vinegar
2½–3 cups vegetable stock
2 tablespoons agave
1 can full-fat coconut milk

DIRECTIONS

1 In a large pot, heat 2–3 tablespoons coconut oil.

2 Add garlic, ginger, and chili flakes and sauté over a medium heat for a few minutes, until translucent.

3 Add the kale and stir until it wilts. Add salt and pepper.

4 Add the tahini, vinegar, stock, and agave. Cover and simmer for 30–35 minutes, or until the kale is nice and tender. Uncover and add the coconut milk and simmer for a few more minutes to thicken.

5 Adjust the salt and pepper if needed.

Yucca Frites with Charred Scallion Aioli

2–4 SERVINGS

Yucca frites are, in my opinion, a sexier way to enjoy fries. Frying this root vegetable creates a crispiness that you just don't get from potatoes. The outside is golden and the inside takes on an almost creamy texture. One thing to note is that yucca cannot be consumed raw as it is poisonous. There's no need to stress, but make sure to boil it before frying and wash your hands after handling. Follow these few procedures and you won't regret the finished product.

1 large yucca, peeled and cut into 1 inch (2.5 cm) batons or strips

Vegetable oil, for frying

¼ cup Charred Scallion Aioli (pg 144)

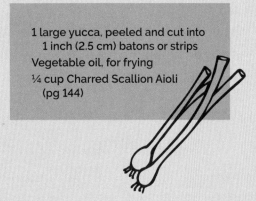

DIRECTIONS

1 Peel the yucca. Cut off the ends and then cut it in half widthwise. Cut each half into thirds, lengthwise. You may have to make a few more cuts depending on the size of the root. They should end up looking like steak fries.

2 Throw them into a large pot of salted boiling water and then reduce to a simmer. (Add a dash of vinegar to the water to help reduce bitterness.) Cook for about 30–35 minutes, drain well, and place onto a paper towel-lined plate.

3 Prepare a frying pan with vegetable oil, so the oil reaches about one-quarter of the way up the side of the pan. Heat the oil over a medium–high heat or, alternatively, prepare a deep-fryer, set at 350°F (175°C).

4 Fry the yucca until crisp and golden brown, about 3–4 minutes, turning halfway if the batons are not submerged in oil.

5 Transfer to a paper towel-lined plate and salt immediately.

SERVE

Serve with the aioli or your favorite dipping sauce.

Tostones/Maduros

2–4 SERVINGS

Alongside rice, fried plantain was the most common staple in my grandmother's house when I was growing up. While most kids I knew ate chips or fries, I ate plantains. The plantain is so common in Puerto Rican cuisine and found its way into most dishes in my family's home. You can fry them when they are green or yellow. Green plantains are unripe and give you a crunchy, savory version of these chips (tostones), while yellow plantains are ripe and, when fried, create lovely sweet bites (maduros).

TOSTONES

1 large green plantain

MADUROS

1 large yellow plantain
Vegetable or olive oil,
  for frying

FOR THE TOSTONES

1 Cut the ends off the plantain then cut a seam lengthwise and peel off the skin. Cut the plantain flesh into 1 inch (2.5 cm) pieces.

2 Heat a frying pan with oil over a medium–high heat. Test the oil with one of the pieces. If it is bubbling, it's good to go. Fry the pieces for 1–2 minutes each side, or just until mostly tender. Pull them out and drain on a paper towel-lined plate.

3 Using a plantain smasher, tortilla press, or the bottom of a plate, smash each piece to about an ⅛ inch (0.5 cm) thick.

4 Add them back to the pan and refry until crispy and golden brown, about 2 minutes, and drain.

SERVE

Salt immediately and serve.

FOR THE MADUROS

1 Prepare the plantains as above, in step 1.

2 Fry for 1–2 minutes over a medium heat, turning halfway if not submerged in the oil. They will get very dark, almost black. This is just the sugars caramelizing and is exactly what you want to happen.

3 Transfer to a paper towel-lined plate.

SERVE

Sprinkle with sugar, cinnamon sugar, or rum syrup. You could even drizzle with chocolate, peanut butter, or whatever creative topping you think of. I enjoy them as they are with rice and beans, or solo as a dessert.

Hearty Proteins

Soyrizo

4–6 SERVINGS

This is my version of chorizo, a Spanish pork sausage that gets its rich, bold, spicy flavor from its star ingredient, paprika. To make a plant-based version, textured vegetable protein can be soaked, drained, and used as a mock meat that will take on any flavor you add to it.

1 cup textured vegetable protein (TVP)

½ tablespoon cumin seeds

1 teaspoon coriander seeds

4 whole cloves (or ⅛ tsp ground cloves)

1-2 bay leaves

2 tablespoons coconut oil

2 tablespoons smoked paprika

½ tablespoon garlic powder

½ tablespoon onion powder

½ teaspoon dried oregano

½ teaspoon dried thyme

¼ teaspoon ground cinnamon

¼ teaspoon cayenne

1 tablespoon apple-cider vinegar

2 tablespoons annatto powder (optional)

½ tablespoon agave

3 cups vegetable stock

DIRECTIONS

1 Soak the TVP in water for about 10 minutes prior to use. Make sure to drain and squeeze out the excess water before cooking.

2 In a small dry pan, toast the cumin and coriander seeds over a medium heat for about 2–4 minutes. They will become fragrant.

3 Remove from the heat and blend in a spice grinder. Also grind the clove and bay leaf. If you don't have a grinder, you can place the clove and bay leaf in a cheesecloth sash, toss in the pan, and remove before serving, and you can crush the toasted cumin and coriander seeds with the back of the pan.

4 Melt the coconut oil in a pan over a medium heat. Add all the ingredients except the TVP and vegetable stock. Stir well to form a paste. Cook for just a few minutes to combine all the flavors.

5 Add the pre-soaked TVP to the pan and stir. Let this cook over a medium–high heat for 4–5 minutes, until the TVP has started to crisp and brown.

6 Add the vegetable stock and cover. Cook for 15–20 minutes, or until the stock has been completely absorbed.

7 Adjust the salt if necessary.

SERVE

Since this has a spicy flavor, I suggest adding it to rice, creamy pastas, salads, nachos, burritos, or maybe a shepherd's pie made with mashed sweet potatoes.

Simple Seitan

4–6 SERVINGS

Now, I am far from an expert on the art of seitan, but to keep things simple, you are kneading a liquid together with vital wheat gluten, the essential ingredient for creating this glorious meat substitute. I can't justify buying ready-made seitan from the store when it is truly so easy to make yourself. Plus, doing so will save you a few bucks while you're at it. You can bake it, steam it, or boil it, and then use it as a base protein that can be cubed, sliced, shredded, ground and so on.

1½ cups vital wheat gluten

¼ cup chickpea flour (besan)

2 tablespoons nootch (nutritional yeast)

1 teaspoon garlic powder

1 teaspoon paprika

1 teaspoon onion powder

¼ teaspoon dried thyme

1 tablespoon liquid aminos

1 cup vegetable broth

2 tablespoons tomato paste

1 tablespoon olive oil

2 garlic cloves, smashed into a paste

DIRECTIONS

1 Preheat the oven to 375°F (190°C).

2 In a mixing bowl, combine the vital wheat gluten, chickpea flour, nootch, and dry spices.

3 In a separate bowl, whisk together the liquid aminos, broth, tomato paste, olive oil, and garlic paste.

4 Pour the liquid mixture into the dry and knead for about 5–10 minutes, forming a ball. The longer you knead, the meatier the texture.

5 Form this mixture into a log shape and wrap completely in parchment paper and then in aluminum foil.

6 Bake for 50 minutes.

SERVE

Once cooled, cube the seitan and throw it in a stir fry or slice it for sandwiches.

"I encourage you to remix these recipes. They are all simply templates to riff off. To me, that's the ultimate way to cook."

Hibiscus Flower Birria Tacos

THIS RECIPE YIELDS ABOUT 6–7 TACOS BUT A LOT OF SAUCE. YOU CAN CUT THE SAUCE RECIPE IN HALF OR USE IT IN SOUPS, STEWS, OR AS A BRAISING LIQUID FOR YOUR OTHER MOCK MEATS.

 Can be gluten free when made with all-corn tortillas

I am impressed with this dish because you are using a flower in place of braised meat. Meat eaters might use a short rib or brisket here, but the hibiscus flower is a believable substitute that takes on that shredded meatiness. It stands up to the bold flavors from the charred vegetables, chilis, and smoked paprika. Slap this goodness into a warm tortilla with cheese. Oh, but we're not done yet! We then dip this fried taco into a rich broth. This one brings a tear of joy to my eye.

1 cup dried hibiscus flowers
2 tablespoons white vinegar
1 tomato, peeled
1 onion, halved
4 garlic cloves, smashed
3 dried guajillo chilis
2 dried pasilla, morita, or ancho chilis
1 chipotle in adobo sauce
1 cup Annatto Oil (pg 152)
1 cup vegetable broth
1 bay leaf

½ tablespoon dried Mexican oregano (regular oregano also works)
4 teaspoons cumin seeds
1 teaspoon coriander seeds
1 teaspoon smoked paprika
1 tablespoon tomato paste
1 tablespoon vegetable oil
1 teaspoon pepper
1 teaspoon paprika
1 teaspoon garlic powder

FOR TOPPING

Favorite tortillas
Vegan mozzarella shreds
Fresh cilantro (coriander), chopped
1 small onion, minced

"This one brings a tear of joy to my eye."

DIRECTIONS

1 Preheat the broiler (grill).

2 Prepare the hibiscus by first rinsing thoroughly with water. Next, bring a pot of water to the boil, add the flowers and cook for about 5 minutes. Add 1 tablespoon of the vinegar to help cut down on the bitterness and tang of the flower.

3 Drain and squeeze out as much excess water as you can.

4 Cut the heat, cover the pot, and let everything steep for 30 minutes.

5 While the hibiscus steeps, place the tomato, onion, and garlic on a foil-lined pan and drizzle with oil and salt. Broil for 5–8 minutes, or until charred and fragrant. Set aside.

6 Drain and squeeze out the excess liquid from the steeped hibiscus, let dry, and then reserve until ready to use.

7 Add the dried chilis to a pot of water. Boil them for 3–4 minutes or until tender. Remove the stems and seeds of the chilis, or leave the seeds if you want a spicier dish.

8 Add the chilis and chili water to a blender with the chipotles in adobo and charred tomato, garlic, and onion mix. Make sure to add any oil that's collected on the foil to the blender as it's full of flavor. Blend until smooth.

9 Add half of the Annatto Oil to a large saucepan, along with the remaining vinegar, broth, chili puree, dried spices (bay leaf, oregano, 3 teaspoons of cumin, coriander, and paprika) tomato paste, and 3 cups of water.

10 Cover and simmer for 20–25 minutes. It should thicken.

11 In a clean sauté pan, sauté the hibiscus flower with oil, salt, pepper, 1 teaspoon of cumin, paprika, and garlic powder.

12 Cook over a medium–high heat for 5 minutes.

13 Add 1–2 cups of the broth and simmer until the sauce is fully incorporated and tender.

TO ASSEMBLE

1 Heat the tortillas by dipping them in the remaining annatto oil and placing on a hot flattop or a large sauté pan or skillet.

2 Spoon the hibiscus and some of the mozzarella into each tortilla shell.

3 Fold the taco and press, allowing both sides to sear and crisp up, about 1 minute each side.

4 Repeat this with all of the filling and top with mozzarella, chopped cilantro and minced onion.

SERVE

Plate with a bowl of the sauce on the side for dipping.

"One day, I turned to Abi and asked her thoughts about living in a van and traveling indefinitely. Without hesitation, she was all in."

Coconut Bacon

2–4 SERVINGS

This recipe came from my wife. She whipped it up one day and I was hooked. You truly get the smoky, savory flavor of crispy bacon without the extra calories. Add to the C.B.L.T. sandwich in this book, to any salad of your choice, as a brunch side, or wherever you want a smoky crunch.

1 tablespoon coconut oil

½ cup unsweetened coconut chips (make sure to get chips, not flakes!)

¼ teaspoon smoked paprika

¼ teaspoon garlic powder

¼ teaspoon onion powder

1 tablespoon nootch (nutritional yeast)

2 teaspoons liquid aminos

1 teaspoon liquid smoke

1 teaspoon maple syrup

DIRECTIONS

1 Add the coconut oil to a medium saucepan. Toast the chips over a medium heat, stirring occasionally, until golden brown, about 5–7 minutes. The chips can burn easily so make sure to stir often and lower the heat if needed.

2 Add all the dry ingredients and stir until everything is evenly incorporated.

3 Turn up the heat slightly and add the liquid smoke and liquid aminos. Cook until the liquid has been absorbed.

4 Immediately cut the heat and add the maple syrup. Mix well and transfer to a paper towel-lined plate. Adjust the salt if needed. Make sure to spread them evenly on a paper towel so they stay crispy.

"Coconut milk, orange, sofrito, garlic, agave, and onion are staples in many of these recipes. I have an affinity for these ingredients: they are my spirit ingredients and elements of my love language."

Mushroom Carnitas

2–4 SERVINGS

As a vegan, one of the dishes I miss most is carnitas. I've had to find a nice alternative so I can still enjoy that rich braised broth, and I can tell you these mushrooms are earth candy. Enjoy the citrusy, bold flavor and be astounded by that texture. If you still want real meat, you may want to bump up the quantity of spices here to compensate. I serve this recipe along with the gnocchi in this book (pg 63), which take on the unique flavor of smoky and sweet.

1 lb (450 g) king oyster mushrooms

1 small onion, diced small

3 garlic cloves, smashed and minced

Olive oil, for sautéing

¾ teaspoon onion powder

1 teaspoon paprika

½ teaspoon ground coriander

1 teaspoon porcini powder

¼ teaspoon chili flakes

½ teaspoon dried Mexican oregano (regular oregano works)

Juice of 1 orange, ¼ teaspoon orange zest

Juice of 1 lime

A few dashes of liquid smoke

DIRECTIONS

1 Cut the ends off the mushroom stems and discard. Cut the caps of the mushrooms and slice them. Take the stalk and shred with a fork. This can seem a bit tricky at first but you'll find your groove.

2 In a big sauté pan, sauté the mushrooms, onion, and garlic in the oil on a medium–high heat.

3 Add the dry spices and let them caramelize for about 5–7 minutes, stirring occasionally.

4 Deglaze the pan with the orange and lime juice, and liquid smoke, and sauté until the liquid has been absorbed.

5 Transfer the mushrooms to a foil-lined pan and bake at 450°F (230°C) for about 20 minutes. They should be a bit crispy.

SERVE

Now you're ready to put them on pretty much anything… tacos, salad, rice, noodles, lettuce wraps, or nachos.

Picadillo "Beefy" Stew with Raisins & Green Olives

4–6 SERVINGS

This dish was commonplace in my household growing up. I enjoyed it served over rice but you can also add to taco salads, burritos, noodles, or as a filling in empanadas. Raisins and green olives are a big part of Puerto Rican cuisine and give this dish a sweetness and tang that round the flavor out perfectly, especially when paired with the tomato. It's like my people knew what they were doing in the kitchen!

Olive oil, for sautéing

1 small yellow onion, diced small

3 garlic cloves, smashed

½ bell pepper (capsicum), diced small

1 cup Sofrito (pg 139)

1 cup textured vegetable protein (TVP), soaked for 10 minutes and drained

1 tablespoon tomato paste

1 tablespoon Nikki Mix (pg 152)

1 small can chopped stewed tomatoes

2–3 cups vegetable stock

¼ cup olives, pitted and chopped

¼ cup raisins, chopped

A handful of fresh cilantro (coriander), chopped

DIRECTIONS

1 To a large saucepan, add the olive oil and sauté the onion, garlic, and pepper with the sofrito for a few minutes.

2 Add the pre-soaked TVP, tomato paste, and spices. Sauté for a few minutes to allow the ingredients to toast.

3 Add the canned tomatoes and stock.

4 Cover and simmer for about 15–20 minutes, or until the stock has absorbed and the TVP is nice and soft.

5 Once you cut the heat, add the chopped raisins and olives and stir to incorporate.

6 Adjust the salt if necessary.

"I credit my grandmother with my affinity for cooking and my desire to make it my career."

Albóndigas Guisadas: No-Meat Meatballs Stewed in Sofrito

4–6 SERVINGS

These Puerto Rican-style no-meat meatballs pack in a lot of flavor. Sofrito plays a big role in the flavor profile and you can do a lot with them. Whichever way you choose to enjoy them, they will become a fan favorite among your family and friends.

SAUCE

¼ cup olive oil

1 small onion, diced small

1 red bell pepper (capsicum), diced small

2 garlic cloves, minced

½ teaspoon dried oregano

¼ teaspoon smoked paprika

1 teaspoon garlic powder

1 teaspoon onion powder

¼ teaspoon ground coriander

1 teaspoon Nikki Mix (pg 152)

¼ teaspoon ground cumin

2 tablespoons Sofrito (pg 139)

1 tablespoon tomato paste

1 can stewed tomatoes

¼ cup red wine

2–3 cups vegetable stock

¼ cup Manzanilla olives, chopped

MEATBALLS

1 shallot, diced small

1 lb (450 g) favorite vegan ground "beef"

½ cup unseasoned breadcrumbs

¼ cup fresh cilantro (coriander), chopped

3 garlic cloves, smashed

1 tablespoon Sofrito (pg 139)

½ teaspoon dried oregano

1 teaspoon ground cumin

FOR SAUCE

1 Add the oil to a large pot and sauté the onion, pepper, garlic, dried spices (oregano, smoked paprika, garlic powder, onion powder, ground coriander, ground cumin) and Nikki mix for 3–4 minutes.

2 Add the sofrito, tomato paste, and canned stewed tomatoes and sauté for another few minutes.

3 Deglaze with the red wine and then add the stock.

4 Cover and simmer for 15 minutes, or until slightly thickened. Once you've cut the heat, add the olives. Adjust the salt if necessary.

FOR MEATBALLS

1 Preheat the oven to 375°F (190°C).

2 Sauté the shallot with a little oil in a small saucepan over a medium heat for about 5 minutes.

3 Add to a medium mixing bowl with the remaining ingredients. Fold until just incorporated (do not over-mix).

4 Use a scoop or your hands to form approximately 1 ounce (30 g) meatballs.

5 In a large sauté pan, sear the meatballs over a medium–high heat, turning until all sides are browned.

6 Add the sauce to the pan and transfer the pan to the oven. Bake for 10–12 minutes.

SERVE

Stack these babies on a hoagie roll, use to top rice or noodles, or serve with a big piece of crusty bread.

Campfire Eats

Whole Roasted Cauliflower with Garlic & Creamy Chipotle Sauce

4–6 SERVINGS

There are so many ways to prepare cauliflower. I appreciate being able to turn it into a puree, a pizza crust, pasta, and so on, but we shouldn't let all these possibilities detract from how lovely this vegetable is on its own. So, this recipe is an ode to the simplicity of cauliflower. You can serve it tableside, on a big platter of your choosing, and with whatever side dishes you want. You can control the spice level by adding more or less chipotle. The sauce gives a richness to the otherwise light flavor profile of the cauliflower.

CHIPOTLE SAUCE

2–3 chipotles, dried (can also use canned)
2 garlic cloves
Juice of ½ orange
Squeeze of lime juice
1 tablespoon agave
¾ cup mayonnaise
Reserved chipotle water, to thin

CAULIFLOWER

1 medium cauliflower
1 small bulb of garlic
⅛ cup oil, for basting
2 teaspoons paprika
2 teaspoons salt
1 teaspoon pepper

DIRECTIONS

1 Boil the chipotles in a small pot of water until tender, about 4–5 minutes. Drain the chilis and reserve the water. Cut off the stems and discard the seeds. Roughly chop them and throw them into a blender or food processor with the remaining sauce ingredients and blend until smooth. Add some of the chili water to thin as desired.

2 Blanch the cauliflower in a large pot of well-salted boiling water for 3–4 minutes, drain, and pat dry. Trim the stem but be careful not to cut too deep as it will fall apart.

3 Mix the oil with the paprika, salt, and pepper to make a paste, and baste the cauliflower.

4 Wrap the cauliflower and garlic in aluminum foil and place in the hot coals of a campfire or bake in your oven at 375°F (190°C) for about an hour. If cooking on a campfire, the cooking time will vary so rotate the cauliflower and check it two or three times to ensure the heat is evenly distributed. Cooking on an open flame is more of a labor of love but it will bring another level of flavor to the char.

5 Unwrap the foil and remove the garlic cloves from their skins. Baste the cauliflower with the creamy garlic cloves and chipotle sauce two or three times throughout the cooking process. Continue to bake for another 10–15 minutes, or until golden and tender, to the point at which a knife can pierce through it.

SERVE

Serve with the remaining sauce and rice, potatoes, or a nice pita or naan bread. I suggest toasting some flatbread and eating it by hand, with some chopped fresh cilantro (coriander) and scallion (spring onion).

"So, this recipe is an ode to the simplicity of cauliflower."

Sexy 'Shrooms

4–6 SERVINGS

Mushrooms have got to be the most intriguing ingredient I work with. There are what seems like endless varieties, all with their own unique flavor profiles, textures, and ideal cooking styles. I finally got my hands on a lion's mane at the farmers' market in San Diego and my life changed. They are one of the best meat alternatives I've found and the best part is they're all natural, with no processed additives.

This recipe highlights the mushroom's texture, creating a super juicy "meaty" dish that reminds me of eating fried chicken as a kid in the south. To me, the chicken was just a vehicle to enjoy the fried batter but now, I enjoy the mushroom just as much. Feed this to your meat-eating friends and I wouldn't be surprised if they couldn't tell the difference.

Vegetable or avocado oil, for shallow-frying
10–12 oz (280–340 g) lion's mane or trumpet mushrooms

WET BATTER

1 cup unsweetened plant-based milk (I use soy or cashew)
¼ cup of your favorite egg alternative (pg 10 and 12)
1 tablespoon apple-cider vinegar
A splash of pickle vinegar
Dash of hot sauce
Dash of liquid smoke

DRY BATTER

2¼ cups all-purpose (plain) flour
2 tablespoons Nikki Mix (pg 152)
Pinch of chili powder
Pinch of mustard powder

DIRECTIONS

1 Tear the lion's mane mushrooms into 1–2 inch (2.5–5 cm) chunks. Make sure they are all around the same size but don't worry about perfection. If you are using trumpet mushrooms, cut them in half, lengthwise.

2 Prepare your dredging station. In one bowl, mix all the wet batter ingredients. You are creating a "buttermilk" with the addition of the vinegar, which will make the batter curdle so stir it right before adding the mushrooms. In another bowl, add all the dry ingredients. Season nicely with salt. Don't be afraid to taste the batters for salt as you want these mushrooms to shine. Finally, prepare a paper towel-lined plate.

3 Prep a sauté pan with the oil over a medium–high heat, adding enough oil to reach at least ¼ inch (0.5 cm) up the side of the pan. Alternatively, prep a deep-fryer to 350°F (175°C).

4 While the oil is heating, grab your mushroom pieces and dip first into the wet batter, then into the dry batter. Repeat the process once, creating a nice coating on each mushroom. Add to the fryer immediately after coating and allow to fry 4–5 minutes per side, or until the batter is nice and golden brown. Repeat with all the pieces and transfer to the paper towel-lined plate.

5 Taste one to see if any more salt is needed.

SERVE

These would be excellent as a fried mushroom sandwich or on top of a salad, in a wrap, as the main star for dinner, or as anything really. They are just damn good. Any sauce in this book would be a great dipper, or make a glaze to toss them in it. Whatever your heart desires.

Twice-Cooked Fingerling Potatoes with Charred Scallion Aioli

2–4 SERVINGS

There is something so satisfying about a crispy potato. It's a staple in almost every household and such a humble ingredient but capable of being the star of endless dishes. Here, I am highlighting the fingerling potato. By boiling it, smashing it, and frying it, you get this crispy outside and tender inside. It's basically the cooler sibling of the French fry.

2 lb (900 g) fingerling (kipfler) potatoes
Vegetable oil, for shallow-frying
Charred Scallion Aioli (pg 144)

DIRECTIONS

1 Boil the potatoes in a large pot of water until fork-tender, about 15–20 minutes.

2 Drain and let them cool slightly. Use the bottom of a plate or a tortilla press and smash them into flat disks, about ¼ inch (0.5 cm) thick. Don't smash them too thin or they will break.

3 Pour enough oil to reach ¼ inch (0.5 cm) up the side of a large frying pan and heat over a medium–high to high heat. Alternatively, prepare a deep-fryer to 350°F (175°C).

4 In batches, add the potatoes to the pan and allow them to cook for 2–3 minutes on each side, or until brown and crispy.

5 Remove from the oil with a slotted spoon and allow to drain on a paper towel-lined plate. Immediately sprinkle them with salt. If you're making a large batch, set the oven to 200°F (90°C) and keep them warm while frying the remaining potatoes.

SERVE

Dip them into the scallion aioli, or dollop the aioli on top.

"I have always considered cooking to be a creative outlet, so following a recipe to the T is not my style."

Nachos with Soyrizo & Smoky Poblano Queso

4–6 SERVINGS

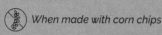 *When made with corn chips*

Who doesn't love nachos? You are basically using chips as a vehicle for scooping up your favorite flavors. Like pizza, nachos can take on pretty much any ingredient. This version takes the slightly spicy Soyrizo (pg 84) and marries it with a creamy garlicky queso. Feel free to add any other salsas, lettuces, condiments, and herbs you'd like. This recipe takes me right back to camping off Colorado's Million Dollar Highway. If you get a chance to drive that route, please do. It is breathtaking. Oh, and stop to make these nachos.

Tortilla chips
Soyrizo (pg 84)

QUESO

1 large poblano chili, destemmed, deseeded, and chopped medium
1 scallion (spring onion)
2 cloves garlic, smashed and minced
1 tablespoon fresh cilantro (coriander), chopped
2 cups plant-based reduced-fat milk
1½ cups of your favorite vegan melty cheese

DIRECTIONS

1   Heat the poblano, scallion, garlic, and cilantro in an oiled cast-iron pan on your stovetop over a medium–high heat. Cook for 3–5 minutes, or until softened.

2   Add your milk. Once it comes to the boil, reduce the heat and simmer. Let it thicken for about 5 minutes.

3   Cut the heat and add your cheese. Stir until it has melted completely. Adjust the seasoning.

4   Arrange your favorite tortilla chips on a foil-lined sheet tray.

5   Ladle on the queso and spread the soyrizo evenly over the chips.

SERVE

Add any and all the toppings you want. I'm excited for you.

"Add any and all the toppings you want.
I'm excited for you."

Grilled Tempeh Kabobs with Miso Plum Glaze

MAKES 6 KABOBS

 But make sure wheat has not been added to the tempeh

This is a sweet, tangy sauce that takes on the char of the grill, symbiotically. The grill gives the tempeh that slow-cooked BBQ flavor. The tempeh is great on its own or as part of a full meal. Have it with rice or roasted potatoes, or slide the skewer into a taco. Keep piling the sauce on. In fact, just triple this glaze recipe. It's addictive. I also advise cutting open an orange, grilling it, and squeezing it over your kabob.

GLAZE

1 teaspoon sesame oil

Large garlic clove, smashed into a paste

1 teaspoon grated ginger

1 tablespoon white miso paste

½ tablespoon hoisin sauce

2 tablespoons plum glaze or jam

2 teaspoons rice-wine vinegar

KABOBS

8 oz (225 g) tempeh, cut into 1 inch (2.5 cm) cubes

½ red bell pepper (capsicum), cut into 1 inch (2.5 cm) squares

¼ red onion, cut into 1 inch (2.5 cm) squares

10–12 cherry tomatoes

DIRECTIONS

1 If using wooden skewers, soak them in water overnight or for a few hours prior to grilling.

2 To make the sauce, in a small saucepan, add the sesame oil, garlic, and ginger. Sauté over a medium heat for about 5 minutes, or until the ginger and garlic are tender and fragrant.

3 Add 2 tablespoons of water and remaining sauce ingredients and bring to the boil, then reduce the heat to a simmer and cook for 4–5 minutes, or until sauce gets thick and bubbly. Allow to cool slightly.

4 Bring a pot of water to the boil and then reduce to a simmer and add the tempeh. Cover and allow to simmer for 5 minutes.

5 Drain the tempeh, pat it dry, and dredge it in the plum sauce. Leave to marinate for 30 minutes.

6 Add pieces of tempeh and vegetables to each skewer, alternating. I was able to get three pieces of tempeh on a medium-sized skewer, making six kabobs.

7 Prep a broiler (grill) or griddle to high, or use the grate over an open fire. Add the skewers and grill for 4–5 minutes per side on a high heat. Make sure to rotate a few times. The tempeh and vegetables should have a nice char and the vegetables should be tender.

SERVE

Serve with rice, noodles, potatoes, or a salad.

Drinks

Saffron Pineapple Lemonade

2–4 SERVINGS

I love these three ingredients and wanted to share a refreshing drink that is excellent as a mocktail in the warmer seasons and still dynamic enough to add your favorite spirit to and enjoy at any time of year. These flavors were inspired by a curry I once made with lemon and saffron. I liked the idea of adding pineapple, and it sure paid off! This is my new favorite refresher and might be yours, too.

Ice

¼ teaspoon saffron threads

16 oz (500 ml) of your favorite lemonade

2 oz (55 g) pineapple chunks (preferably fresh)

DIRECTIONS

Add ice to your favorite cup and blend the remaining ingredients in a high-speed blender. Add more lemonade for a tangier experience, or more pineapple for a thicker drink.

Aguave Limonada

1 SERVE

I have always been a fan of limeade and it's even more exciting when paired with guava. This refresher can be enjoyed as a mocktail or, if you want a cocktail, I suggest adding your favorite vodka, rum, or mezcal.

AGUAVE SIMPLE SYRUP

¼ cup guava jam

Dash of agave

LIMONADA

Ice

1 fl oz (30 ml) favorite liquor (optional)

½ fl oz (15 ml) fresh lime juice

2 fl oz (60 ml) Aguave Simple Syrup (see left)

3 fl oz (90 ml) lemonade or limeade

DIRECTIONS

1 In a small saucepan, bring the guava jam, agave and ¾ cup of water to a simmer on the stovetop.

2 Reduce the heat for about 5 minutes or until the mixture has slightly thickened, forming a syrup. Cut the heat and let it cool completely.

3 Prepare your rocks glass with ice.

4 If adding alcohol, pour a 1-oz jigger of an alcohol of your choice in the glass, followed by the remaining ingredients.

5 Stir and enjoy!

"I hope you can find more than just recipes in these pages. Whether it is a connection to your own nostalgia, inspiration to hit the road, or a desire to pursue your ultimate passions and live your life in a way that lights your soul on fire."

Sweet Corn Drink

2–4 SERVINGS

This drink is inspired by the Central American drink Atole de Elote. Two women who worked as prep crew at one of the first restaurants I worked at used to make this for the kitchen staff and I fell in love with it. There is something so soothing and satisfying about a creamy sweet beverage, and this one is unique and moreish. Here, I added a bit of spice and nutmeg to enhance the flavor. This could also be a base for an ice cream.

2 ears sweet corn

2 cups full-fat coconut milk, or your favorite plant-based milk

1 cinnamon stick or ½ teaspoon ground cinnamon

⅛ teaspoon ground nutmeg

Pinch of cayenne (optional)

1 tablespoon agave

DIRECTIONS

1 Shuck the uncooked corn and add to a high-speed blender with half of the milk and blitz until smooth.

2 Transfer to a pot with the remaining ingredients, including the rest of the milk, bringing it to a boil and then down to a simmer.

3 Simmer, stirring often, for about 12–15 minutes, or until it has started to thicken slightly. Strain through cheesecloth or a fine-mesh strainer. Serve warm.

Avocado Coquito with Miso Caramel

4–6 SERVINGS

Coquito is a divine, creamy coconut rum drink from Puerto Rico. I wanted to take the creaminess a step further by adding avocado, and top it with miso caramel, giving it a sweet/salty touch. I omitted the alcohol to keep this as a mocktail but feel free to add some, particularly rum. This would be excellent as a dessert drink as it is heavier.

MISO CARAMEL

1 cup raw sugar

¾ cup your favorite nut milk

⅛ teaspoon vanilla extract

1 tablespoon white miso paste

AVOCADO COQUITO

1 can full-fat unsweetened coconut milk

1½–2 cups your favorite plant-based milk

1 teaspoon ground cinnamon

⅛ teaspoon ground nutmeg

Pinch of ground cloves

¼ cup agave or your favorite sweetener

1 small avocado, pitted and roughly chopped

FOR THE MISO CARAMEL

1 In a medium non-stick sauté pan, add the sugar and cook over a medium–low heat. Don't stir!

2 Once you see the sugar start to melt and turn golden brown, tilt the pan in circles, moving the sugar slightly so it doesn't burn. If it is getting too dark, cut the heat to low. This is a slow process, so enjoy it!

3 Once most of the sugar is caramelized, start to gently stir it, ensuring all the sugar is dissolved.

4 Turn the heat up to medium and quickly whisk in the milk. Make sure the milk is at room temperature or the caramel will seize up. Whisk it quickly so it doesn't start to clump together. Keep stirring until the caramel starts to smoothen out again. This will take some time.

5 Once the caramel is silky, cut the heat and add the vanilla, miso, and a pinch of salt. Stir it until it is completely incorporated. Store in a squeezy bottle for up to 2 weeks.

FOR THE AVOCADO COQUITO

1 Make sure all of the ingredients are chilled.

2 Add them to a blender and blend at a high speed until smooth. You may add more milk if you'd prefer a thinner drink.

SERVE

Pour into your favorite glasses, drizzle with the caramel and enjoy!

"I make one of these teas every morning and sit with the warm mug in my hand expressing one thing I am grateful for and setting my intention for the day."

Golden Milk Tea

1 SERVE

Throughout my journey on the road, I have felt a primordial call to unearth parts of myself I didn't know needed a voice. In making the decision to go on a spiritual, healing, deep dive, I feel more at home than I ever have before. Along with this shift in consciousness, I wanted to celebrate my well-being and healthy practices, and switching my morning coffee for this drink was the first step. It represents the little things that can shape the bigger picture. I make one of these teas every morning and sit with the warm mug in my hand, expressing one thing I am grateful for and setting my intention for the day.

This drink is a representation of a culmination of travel, insight, experience, and transformation.

If you are feeling called to dig deeper into self-evaluation, I applaud you. We are all here just trying to get to the root of love. While you're on that journey, whatever it looks like, know you are not alone and that I am raising my mug of tea to you, toasting your journey.

1 packet of your favorite black tea
(I use tea bags)
Hot water
Pinch of ground turmeric
Pinch of ground cardamom
Pinch of ground cinnamon
Pinch of ground nutmeg
Pinch of ground black pepper
Small knob of ginger, smashed
Favorite plant-based milk
Agave, to taste

DIRECTIONS

Add all of the ingredients to your mug except the milk and agave. Steep for 3–4 minutes. Stir in the milk and agave. I like to leave the ginger in as it adds more flavor over time.

Sauces, Butters & Seasonings

Queso

6–8 SERVINGS

This queso is made completely from vegetables! Have as much as you like without any guilt. I wanted a lighter option that was nut free and didn't sacrifice any flavor. Top your Seitan Philly (pg 22), nachos (pg 113), or anything your heart desires with this.

1 small russet potato, diced medium

1 medium carrot, roughly chopped

1 small yellow onion, roughly chopped

1 small jalapeño, deseeded and minced (optional)

1–2 garlic cloves

1 cup nootch (nutritional yeast)

¼ teaspoon onion powder

¼ teaspoon garlic powder

¼ teaspoon ground cumin

Pinch of turmeric for color (optional)

¼ cup vegan half-and-half (low-fat) or your favorite plant-based milk (I recommend oat or cashew as they're creamier)

A squeeze of fresh lemon juice

DIRECTIONS

1 Boil the potato, carrot, and onion in a medium pot of salted water, with enough water just to cover the vegetables.

2 Cook until all the vegetables are completely tender, about 5–7 minutes.

3 Drain but reserve about 1 cup of the cooking liquid.

4 Add the vegetables, jalapeño, garlic, nootch and spices and half the reserved water to a high-speed blender. Blend until smooth. Add more water if the sauce seems too thick.

5 Transfer to a clean pot. Add the milk and simmer for a few minutes.

6 Once you turn off the heat, add the lemon juice and adjust the salt if necessary.

"If you are feeling called to dig deeper into self-evaluation, I applaud you. We are all here just trying to get to the root of love."

Sofrito

YIELDS A LOT!

This recipe right here was the aromatic base for most of the cooking done at my grandma's house. It is, in my opinion, a quintessential flavor in Puerto Rican cooking, and it's always necessary if you want the dishes to taste authentic. Use it as a base in rice dishes, soups, and sauces.

1 yellow onion, roughly chopped

1 bell pepper (capsicum), roughly chopped

1 hot chili pepper of your choice (I use serrano), deseeded and roughly chopped★

1 tablespoon Aji Amarillo paste (pg 143)★★

2 mini sweet peppers (such as pimento or cherry), deseeded and roughly chopped

5 garlic cloves

1 bunch of fresh cilantro (coriander), including stems, rinsed and roughly chopped

1 large tomato, or 3 Roma tomatoes, cored and chopped

2–3 culantro (long-leafed coriander) leaves (if you can't find these, just add more cilantro)

★ If you'd like a less spicy version, omit the hot chili pepper.

★★ If you can't find this, just double the amount of sweet pepper.

DIRECTIONS

1 Blend all of the ingredients together in a food processor or high-speed blender.

2 Freeze it in ice-cube trays for up to 6 months, or store for up to 1 week in the fridge.

"For those who love the taste of chilis but are not fond of too much spice, this is for you."

Poblano Aioli

6–8 SERVINGS

The poblano chili has a unique flavor with a mild spice level, which makes this aioli creamy, cool, and versatile. Its heat level won't overpower the overall flavor of whatever dish you use it on. For those who love the taste of chilis but are not fond of too much spice, this is for you. Add this to sandwiches, nachos, rice dishes, or use as a dip for vegetables or potatoes.

1–2 poblano peppers, depending on size

1 small jalapeño (optional, omit if you want this aioli less spicy)

2–3 garlic cloves, smashed

1 squeeze lime juice

1 cup mayonnaise

DIRECTIONS

1   Roast the poblano peppers (and jalapeño, if using), on an open flame or in the oven at 400°F (200°C) for 10–15 minutes until almost completely black.

2   Sauté the garlic in a small oiled pan for a few minutes to soften and release the flavor.

3   Peel away some of the blackened skin from the peppers, cut off the stems, remove the seeds, roughly chop, and add to a food processor, along with the garlic and remaining ingredients and blend until smooth. If too thick, add a bit of water.

Aji Amarillo Aioli

6–8 SERVINGS

In case you haven't yet noticed, I'm a fan of flavored creamy condiments. As I use a lot of acid and spice in many of my dishes, I find that the creaminess of aioli balances these components well. Here, the use of the Aji Amarillo paste gives this aioli a bright yellow hue that creates a stunning aesthetic to any dish it's part of.

2 tablespoons Aji Amarillo paste (or roasted yellow pepper/ capsicum, minced)

Juice of ½ orange

1 cup mayonnaise

½ tablespoon agave

Sprinkle of ground turmeric to enhance the color

DIRECTIONS

1   Mix all the ingredients in a bowl (with salt to taste).

2   Put it on stuff.

3   Literally, that's it.

Charred Scallion Aioli

6–8 SERVINGS

I first tried out this aioli at my last job before I took off in the van. One of my co-worker's parents were coming in for the night and he wanted to make a progressive meal "off menu," meaning something that couldn't be ordered usually. We decided to pair this aioli with some empanadas and it was a crowd pleaser. The char on the scallions (spring onions) gives a depth of flavor. You can use this as a base aioli and add other herbs if you wish.

1 bunch (8–10) scallions (spring onions)
3–4 garlic cloves, smashed
½ tablespoon olive oil
1 cup mayonnaise
A squeeze of lemon juice

DIRECTIONS

1 Toss the scallions in some oil and a sprinkle of salt. Using your oven's broil (grill) setting, char the scallions until they start to turn black, about 4–5 minutes.

2 Meanwhile, sauté the smashed garlic in the oil in a small pan until soft, about 5 minutes.

3 Chop the ends off the scallions, roughly chop, and add to a food processor with the remaining ingredients.

4 Blend until smooth and adjust the seasoning if necessary. You may need to add a bit of water to thin the aioli out.

Chimichurri Rojo

6–8 SERVINGS

This is my take on the condiment that originates from Argentina. I love the robust flavor and color combination of this sauce, and it pairs well with mock meats, rice, and potatoes. For a snack, just toast some of your favorite bread and dip on in.

1 cup roasted red pepper (capsicum), finely chopped

⅛ cup fresh parsley, finely chopped

1 tablespoon fresh cilantro (coriander), finely chopped

½ teaspoon smoked paprika

Pinch of red chili flakes

2 garlic cloves, smashed and minced

⅛ teaspoon orange zest

1 tablespoon olive oil

DIRECTIONS

Add all the ingredients to a bowl and mix well.

"Feel free to alter the recipes to suit your way of eating. I am simply creating a foundation of flavor for you to build upon."

Mock Mole

YIELDS A LOT!

I've always admired mole and how complex it is. Originating from Mexico, there seem to be endless varieties and the process of making it is a labor of love. The flavors that build are unlike anything else, and while I want to share that experience, most people don't have the time to spend on the authentic process (which can take a whole day). And, honestly, I'm no expert. Therefore, I've created a quicker, less complex version that I believe still gives those layers of flavor but in less time. The black beans are the base, and help give this version the texture of a true mole. Enjoy this rich sauce on mock meats, grilled veggies, and burritos. I also sometimes love to add vegetable stock to make this into a soup or stew for a cold day.

If you can't get the suggested types of chilis (ancho, guajillo, and morita chilis), use dried pasilla, mulato, poblano, or chipotles instead.

1 dried ancho chili, deseeded and destemmed

3 dried guajillo chilis, deseeded and destemmed

2 dried morita chilis, deseeded and destemmed

1 teaspoon cumin seeds

½ teaspoon coriander seeds

1 teaspoon sesame seeds

¼ cup raisins

2 corn tortillas

½ yellow onion, roughly chopped

4 garlic cloves

1 large tomato, cored and roughly chopped

1 can black beans, with liquid

2–3 cloves

1 cinnamon stick or ½ teaspoon ground cinnamon

⅛ teaspoon ground allspice

½ teaspoon Mexican oregano

1–2 tablespoons agave

2–2½ cups vegetable stock

Juice of 1 orange

1 tablespoon cocoa powder or 1 oz (30 g) 70%+ cacao bar

DIRECTIONS

1 Toast the dried chilis in a sauté pan along with the cumin, coriander, and sesame seeds over medium–high heat for a few minutes, until fragrant and the chilis start to darken.

2 In a high-speed blender, add the dried and toasted chilis, coriander, cumin, sesame seeds, raisins, tortillas, onion, garlic, tomato, and black beans. Blend well until smooth.

3 Transfer the mixture to a large sauté pan or pot and add the cloves, cinnamon stick, allspice, oregano, agave, and stock.

4 Cover and simmer over a medium heat for 30–35 minutes.

5 Uncover and add the orange juice and cocoa powder or cacao.

6 Adjust the salt level if necessary. The sauce should be quite thick.

7 Cut the recipe in half if you don't want to make too much. You can freeze it for up to 6 months.

Sun-Dried Tomato Butter

6–8 SERVINGS

This butter has been a staple in my kitchen for quite some time, ever since working in Italian kitchens for four years. I'm a big believer that bread needs butter but it can't be boring, so make this. I insist.

1 cup butter, unsalted and at room temperature

¾ cup sun-dried tomatoes, drained if packed in oil, and finely chopped

½ teaspoon orange zest

A sprinkle of finely chopped parsley

DIRECTIONS

Fold all the ingredients into the butter. Store in the fridge until ready for use.

"I hope you get the sense that the food is a culmination of my dharma. I am beyond grateful to be able to spread love and humility through cuisine."

Caramelized Scallion Butter

6–8 SERVINGS

This butter is my favorite. Slow cooking the scallion (spring onion) with garlic until it melts is just damn good. Throw it on a grilled cheese, add it to a sauce, spread it on a sandwich, or mix it into some mashed potatoes. It's creamy, oniony goodness.

½ bunch (around 5) scallions (spring onions)
2 garlic cloves, smashed
4 fl oz (115 grams) butter

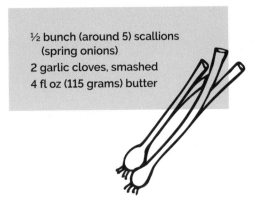

DIRECTIONS

1   Roast the scallions on a griddle, open flame, or on broil (grill) in the oven until they start to wilt and char. Cut off the ends and dice finely.

2   Next, sauté the garlic, scallion, and butter in a small pan. Slowly simmer until soft, about 5–7 minutes.

3   Blend in a small blender or food processor (this is optional but I like the color it lends and it helps meld all of the flavors together. Feel free to leave it rustic with the chunks of melted garlic and scallion intact).

4   Allow to cool and store in the refrigerator until ready for use.

Nikki Mix

MAKES APPROX. 3 TABLESPOONS

This is my version of the traditional Puerto Rican seasoning. This mix is perfect for rice, stews, mock meats, sauces, and more. Along with Sofrito (pg 139), it's a staple ingredient throughout this book.

½ tablespoon cumin
¼ tablespoon ground coriander
1 tablespoon achiote powder
1 tablespoon garlic powder
¼ tablespoon dried oregano
½ tablespoon onion powder
1 teaspoon salt
¼ teaspoon pepper

DIRECTIONS

Mix all the ingredients in a bowl. Store in a sealed container.

Annatto Oil

6–8 SERVINGS

Annatto is the seed of the achiote plant. Oil infused with annatto, when used for cooking, gives dishes a bright red-orange color and a robust flavor that is a bit floral and a bit peppery. Mostly, I enjoy the color and the fact that my grandma used it in many of her dishes. This oil is especially good when making Arroz Mamposteao (Puerto Rican rice and beans; pg 72), Jambalaya (pg 70), and Soyrizo (pg 84), to name just a few dishes.

1 cup vegetable oil
1 tablespoon annatto seeds

DIRECTIONS

1 In a small sauté pan, add the oil and annatto seeds and stir together. Cook over a medium heat for about 5 minutes, or until the oil takes on an intense red color.

2 Turn off the heat and strain out the seeds. Make sure not to cook on too high a heat or the annatto will burn and take on a bitter taste.

3 Store at room temperature.

"Mostly, I enjoy the color and the fact that my grandma used annatto in many of her dishes."

Annatto and Orange Butter

6–8 SERVINGS

Annatto is a seed from an achiote tree and basically is a color additive for dishes. The subtle floral flavor of the annatto pairs beautifully with the sweet citrus of the orange but, in my opinion, its main job is really just to make the food pop. It's what made my grandmother's rice so vibrant and adds to the excitement of this butter.

Juice and zest of 1 orange
1 tsp annatto powder or oil
(pg 152)
4 fl oz (115 grams) butter, unsalted

DIRECTIONS

1 In a small sauté pan, simmer the orange juice for a few minutes to reduce it by half.

2 In a bowl, mix the oil or annatto powder with the butter, orange zest and juice, and salt to taste.

3 Store in the fridge until ready to use.

Index

A

Aguave Limonada 124
aioli
  Aji Amarillo Aioli 143
  Charred Scallion Aioli 76, 110, 144
  Poblano Aioli 143
Aji Amarillo Aioli 143
  C.B.L.T.: Coconut Bacon, Lettuce &
    Tomato Sandwich with Aji Amarillo
    Aioli 27
aji amarillo paste
  Aji Amarillo Aioli 143
  Baked Cabbage Rolls with Picadillo &
    Aji Amarillo Corn Crema 52
Albondigas Guisadas: No-Meat
  Meatballs Stewed in Sofrito 98
Annatto Oil 152
  Annatto and Orange Butter 155
Arroz Mamposteao: Puerto Rican
  Stewed Beans & Rice 72
avocados
  Avocado Coquito with
    Miso Caramel 126
  Guacamole with Caramelized
    Ginger & Orange 55

B

Baked Cabbage Rolls with
  Picadillo & Aji Amarillo Corn
  Crema 52
bananas, Stewed Banana Oatmeal 11
batters
  Dry Batter 107
  Tempura Batter 20–1
  Wet Batter 107
BBQ Sauce 26
Beetroot Vinaigrette 32–3
black beans
  Mock Mole 148
  Refried Black Beans 2–3
black-eyed peas, Coconut Braised
  Black-Eyed Peas 71
Braised Kale with Coconut Milk
  & Tahini 75
Braised Pintos 36
bread
  Coconut Fry Bread 50
  Green chili croutons 38
  Guava-Stuffed French Toast
    with Coconut Syrup 10

broccoletti 32–3
bruschetta, Roasted Strawberry
  Bruschetta 56
burritos, Nat's Ultimate Burritos 34
butternut squash
  Creamy Butternut Squash Pasta,
    Coconut Bacon & Gingersnap
    Crumble 66–7
  Tempura Squash 20–1
butters
  Annatto and Orange Butter 155
  Caramelized Scallion Butter 150
  Sun-Dried Tomato Butter 149

C

cabbage
  Baked Cabbage Rolls with
    Picadillo & Aji Amarillo Corn
    Crema 52
  Napa Cabbage & Orange Salad with
    Chili Pepitas & Creamy Guava
    Vinaigrette 37
  Orange Sesame Slaw 20–1
Caramelized Onions 22
Caramelized Scallion Butter 150
cauliflower, Whole Roasted
  Cauliflower with Garlic &
  Creamy Chipotle Sauce 104
C.B.L.T.: Coconut Bacon, Lettuce &
  Tomato Sandwich with Aji Amarillo
  Aioli 27
Chanterelle & Hazelnut Ramen 40–1
Charred Scallion Aioli 76, 144
  Twice-Cooked Fingerling Potatoes
    with Charred Scallion Aioli 110
Chilaquiles: Tortillas in a Chili
  Simmering Sauce 15
chili
  Chili Pepitas 37
  Chili Simmering Sauce 15
  Green Chili Croutons 38
  Mock Mole 148
Chimichurri Rojo 2–3, 146
Chipotle Sauce 104
Coconut Bacon 94
  C.B.L.T.: Coconut Bacon,
    Lettuce & Tomato Sandwich
    with Aji Amarillo Aioli 27
  Creamy Butternut Squash Pasta,
    Coconut Bacon & Gingersnap
    Crumble 66–7

coconut milk
  Braised Kale with Coconut Milk &
    Tahini 75
  Coconut Braised Black-Eyed Peas 71
  Coconut Fry Bread 50
  Coconut Soup with Pistachio Pesto 45
  Coconut Syrup 10
  Peanut Stew with Sweet Potato
    Peppers & Coconut Milk 47
Creamy Butternut Squash Pasta,
  Coconut Bacon & Gingersnap
  Crumble 66–7
Creamy Ramen Noodles 62
Crispy Mushrooms 22
croutons 38–9
crumble, Gingernut Crumble 66–7

D

dressing
  Beetroot Vinaigrette 32–3
  Guava Vinaigrette 37
  Manchego Dressing 39

E

Empanetzels with Soyrizo & Sweet
  Plantain 53

G

glazes
  Miso Plum Glaze 118
  Strawberry Balsamic Glaze 56
gnocchi, Plantain Gnocchi with
  Meat-Free Mushroom Carnitas 63
Golden Milk Tea 130
green olives, Picadillo "Beefy" Stew
  with Raisins & Green Olives 97
Grilled Romaine Lettuce, Charred
  Tomato, Green Chili Croutons &
  Manchego Dressing 38–9
Grilled Tempeh Kabobs with Miso Plum
  Glaze 118
Guacamole with Caramelized Ginger &
  Orange 55
guava jam
  Aguave Limonada 124
  Guava Cream Cheese 10
  Guava Vinaigrette 37
  Guava-Stuffed French Toast with
    Coconut Syrup 10

guava paste, Tamarind Guava BBQ
 Tempeh Sandwiches 26

H

hazelnuts, Chanterelle & Hazelnut
 Ramen 40–1
Hibiscus Flower Birria Tacos 88–9

K

kabobs, Grilled Tempeh Kabobs with
 Miso Plum Glaze 118
kale, Braised Kale with Coconut Milk &
 Tahini 75
kidney beans, Arroz Mamposteao:
 Puerto Rican Stewed Beans &
 Rice 72
kitchen essentials xiv–xv

L

lemonade
 Aguava Limonada 124
 Saffron Pineapple Lemonade 122
lettuce
 C.B.L.T.: Coconut Bacon, Lettuce &
  Tomato Sandwich with Aji Amarillo
  Aioli 27
 Grilled Romaine Lettuce, Charred
  Tomato, Green Chili Croutons &
  Manchego Dressing 38–9
Loaded Potato Pancakes 12

M

macaroni, Smoked Poblano &
 Manchego Mac 'n' Cheese 64
Maduros 78
Manchego cheese
 Manchego Dressing 38
 Smoked Poblano & Manchego
  Mac 'n' Cheese 64
Masa Cakes Benedict with Smoked
 Tofu, Refried Black Beans &
 Chimichurri Rojo 2–3
meatballs, Albondigas Guisadas:
 No-Meat Meatballs Stewed
 in Sofrito 98
miso paste
 Miso Caramel 126
 Miso Plum Glaze 118

Mock Mole 148
mole, Mock Mole 148
mushrooms
 Chanterelle & Hazelnut
  Ramen 40–1
 Crispy Mushrooms 22
 Mushroom Carnitas 96
 Plantain Gnocchi with Meat-Free
  Mushroom Carnitas 63
 Sexy 'Shrooms 107

N

Nachos with Soyrizo & Smoky Poblano
 Queso 113
Napa Cabbage & Orange Salad with
 Chili Pepitas & Creamy Guava
 Vinaigrette 37
Nat's Ultimate Burritos 36
Nikki Mix 152
noodles see Ramen noodles

O

oats, Stewed Banana Oatmeal 11
onions, Caramelized Onions 22
orange
 Annatto and Orange Butter 155
 Guacamole with Caramelized
  Ginger & Orange 55
 Napa Cabbage & Orange Salad with
  Chili Pepitas & Creamy Guava
  Vinaigrette 37
 Orange Amaretto Sauce 4
 Orange Sesame Slaw 20–1

P

pancakes, Loaded Potato
 Pancakes 12
pasta
 Creamy Butternut Squash Pasta,
  Coconut Bacon & Gingersnap
  Crumble 66–7
 Smoked Poblano & Manchego
  Mac 'n' Cheese 64
Peanut Stew with Sweet Potato
 Peppers & Coconut Milk 47
pepitas, Chili Pepitas 37
pesto
 Pesto Butter 56
 Pistachio Pesto 45

picadillo
 Baked Cabbage Rolls with Picadillo &
  Aji Amarillo Corn Crema 52
 Picadillo "Beefy" Stew with Raisins &
  Green Olives 97
pineapple, Saffron Pineapple
 Lemonade 122
pink beans, Arroz Mamposteao: Puerto
 Rican Stewed Beans & Rice 72
pinto beans, Braised Pintos 36
pistachios, Pistachio Pesto 45
plantains
 Empanetzels with Soyrizo & Sweet
  Plantain 53
 Plantain Gnocchi with Meat-Free
  Mushroom Carnitas 63
 Sweet Risotto with Plantains &
  Orange Amaretto Sauce 4
 Tostones/Maduros 78
 see also bananas
poblano peppers
 Poblano Aioli 143
 Smoked Poblano & Manchego
  Mac 'n' Cheese 64
pomegranate, Salsa 36
potatoes
 Loaded Potato Pancakes 12
 Twice-Cooked Fingerling Potatoes
  with Charred Scallion Aioli 110

Q

Queso 136
 Nachos with Soyrizo & Smoky
  Poblano Queso 113
 Nat's Ultimate Burritos 36

R

raisins, Picadillo "Beefy" Stew with
 Raisins & Green Olives 97
ramen noodles
 Chanterelle & Hazelnut
  Ramen 40–1
 Creamy Ramen Noodles 62
Refried Black Beans 2–3
rice 36
 Arroz Mamposteao: Puerto Rican
  Stewed Beans & Rice 72
 Black Rice 32–3
 Sweet Risotto with Plantains &
  Orange Amaretto Sauce 4

Roasted Strawberry Bruschetta with Pesto Butter & Strawberry Balsamic Glaze 56

Saffron Pineapple Lemonade 122
salads
    Grilled Romaine Lettuce, Charred Tomato, Green Chili Croutons & Manchego Dressing 38–9
    Napa Cabbage & Orange Salad with Chili Pepitas & Creamy Guava Vinaigrette 37
    Superfood Salad with Smoky Tahini Beetroot Vinaigrette 32–3
Salsa 36
sandwiches
    C.B.L.T.: Coconut Bacon, Lettuce & Tomato Sandwich with Aji Amarillo Aioli 27
    Tamarind Guava BBQ Tempeh Sandwiches 26
sauces 70, 98
    BBQ Sauce 20–1
    Chili Simmering Sauce 15
    Chimichurri Rojo 2–3, 146
    Chipotle Sauce 104
    Mock Mole 148
    Orange Amaretto Sauce 4
    Tamarind BBQ Sauce 20–1
scallions
    Caramelized Scallion Butter 150
    Charred Scallion Aioli 76, 110, 144
seitan
    Seitan Philly 22
    Simple Seitan 87
Sexy 'Shrooms 107
Simple Seitan 87
slaw, Orange Sesame Slaw 20–1
Smoked Poblano & Manchego Mac 'n' Cheese 64
Smoked Tofu 2–3
Sofrito 139
    Albondigas Guisadas: No-Meat Meatballs Stewed in Sofrito 98
Some Kinda Jumbled Jambalaya 70
soup, Coconut Soup with Pistachio Pesto 45
Soyrizo 84
    Empanetzels with Soyrizo & Sweet Plantain 53

Nachos with Soyrizo & Smoky Poblano Queso 113
Stewed Banana Oatmeal 11
strawberries
    Roasted Strawberry Bruschetta 56
    Strawberry Balsamic Glaze 56
Sun-Dried Tomato Butter 149
Superfood Salad with Smoky Tahini Beetroot Vinaigrette 32–3
sweet corn
    Masa Cakes 2–3
    Sweet Corn Crema 20–1, 52
    Sweet Corn Drink 124
Sweet Corn Crema
    Baked Cabbage Rolls with Picadillo & Aji Amarillo Corn Crema 52
    Tempura-Fried Squash Tacos with Sweet Corn Crema, Tamarind BBQ Sauce & Orange Sesame Slaw 20–1
sweet potatoes
    Peanut Stew with Sweet Potato Peppers & Coconut Milk 47
    Superfood Salad 32–3
Sweet Risotto with Plantains & Orange Amaretto Sauce 4
syrups
    Aguave Simple Syrup 124
    Coconut Syrup 10

tacos, Hibiscus Flower Birria Tacos 88–9
tahini
    Braised Kale with Coconut Milk & Tahini 75
    Superfood Salad with Smoky Tahini Beetroot Vinaigrette 32–3
Tamarind BBQ Sauce 20–1
Tamarind Guava BBQ Tempeh Sandwiches 26
tea, Golden Milk Tea 130
tempeh 32–3
    Grilled Tempeh Kabobs with Miso Plum Glaze 118
    Tamarind Guava BBQ Tempeh Sandwiches 26
Tempura Batter 20–1
Tempura-Fried Squash Tacos with Sweet Corn Crema, Tamarind BBQ Sauce & Orange Sesame Slaw 20–1

textured vegetable protein (TVP)
    Picadillo "Beefy" Stew with Raisins & Green Olives 97
    Soyrizo 84
toast, Guava-Stuffed French Toast with Coconut Syrup 10
tofu, Smoked Tofu 2–3
tomatoes
    C.B.L.T.: Coconut Bacon, Lettuce & Tomato Sandwich with Aji Amarillo Aioli 27
    Chili Simmering Sauce 15
    Grilled Romaine Lettuce, Charred Tomato, Green Chili Croutons & Manchego Dressing 38–9
    Sun-Dried Tomato Butter 149
tortillas
    Chilaquiles: Tortillas in a Chili Simmering Sauce 15
    Hibiscus Flower Birria Tacos 88–9
    Nachos with Soyrizo & Smoky Poblano Queso 113
Tostones/Maduros 78
Twice-Cooked Fingerling Potatoes with Charred Scallion Aioli 110

vegan sausage, Some Kinda Jumbled Jambalaya 70
vital wheat gluten 87

Wet Batter 107
Whole Roasted Cauliflower with Garlic & Creamy Chipotle Sauce 104

Yucca Frites with Charred Scallion Aioli 76

Acknowledgments

As I sit here writing this page, I feel the tears of gratitude welling up. I have spent over a year working on this project but my whole career, to this point, searching for my true purpose. It has taken me until now to really appreciate my craft, my abilities, and that my ideas are worth sharing. Cooking has been the creative outlet that has really allowed me to speak. So, first, I'm thanking food.

To my grandmother, Matilde, to whom this book is dedicated: I feel your legacy running through my veins every time I pick up that knife and start to create. Every day I have to eat and every day I feel your love.

To my mother, Jeannette, whose superpower I am always channeling: I know you are always with me, lighting my path through this life.

Deb, Harry, and Pepi, my foundation. My family, who have always supported my quirky, out-of-the-box approach to all I do. You may not always understand my choices but you celebrate my unconventional ways of living.

To my wife, Abi, who is my grounded earth and motivator. You have allowed me to become all facets of myself as they arise, and you celebrate me to my fullest. Thank you for letting me feed you, and for being my biggest fan.

To Tawny, for believing in me, housing me, and for letting me experiment and create most of this book in your presence and space. I can't find all the words to express my gratitude for the time you took to help me nurture and edit these pages. Your feedback was raw, and after reading your book I was inspired to do this. Most of all, thank you for making sure I didn't include broccoli dogs in this book.

Thank you to Mike, Ely, Aidyn, Evan and Al for doing your best to keep open minds and palates.

Thank you to Andrew Knapp, for being my initial inspiration to take off on the road to live my life on purpose.

To Joaquin and Naima, for creating magic with me in Baja Mexico and for really inspiring me to see my own potential to create menus.

Thank you to my friends, nomad family, co-workers, chefs, and every person I have had the privilege of feeding, and who listened as I went through the emotions and trials that led me to this point. You know who you are and I am honored to have this book to show for it all. To my soul tribe, Mukbang.

Thank you to Elen, Melissa, Megan, Madeleine, Betsy, and everyone involved with my book at Hardie Grant Publishing for believing in my art. I believe in synchronicity and this incredible team of people came into my life and saw my potential just when I needed to let myself fly.

Finally, I'm going to thank myself. Maybe that's my Leo energy speaking, or perhaps self love. It has taken me most of my life to really, deeply, feel that. I'm proud that I did and am doing the hard work to connect fully with myself and my creativity. I can now look inside and say to myself, "Your poetry and food mean something."

I am a big advocate for mental health and personal growth. Whoever you are, know that what you have inside is a fuel nobody else has, so ignite it. We help others and the world by coming fully alive and sharing what we have so that it may, little by little, shift the overall dynamic of humanity. I'm telling my story in the hope that even just one person can celebrate their own—and also eat a damn good meal in the process.

Thank you.

Natalie Nikki Rodriguez is a professionally trained chef, writer, wife, dog mom, and full-time traveler. Growing up in her Puerto Rican grandmother's kitchen, she has a natural affinity for cooking. She attended the Culinary Institute of Charleston in 2013 and quickly started a career as a chef, working in various kitchens around Charleston, South Carolina. After more than a decade of the food and beverage grind, she felt a relentless pull to travel and to expand her creativity.

She and her wife, Abigail, quit their jobs, sold all of their belongings, and bought a van to travel the country. At that time, pursuing a "vanlife" lifestyle (as depicted in social media) was fairly new, and the idea of cooking in a van didn't seem like a luxury. But they did the research, saved the money, got married, and built the van all within a year-and-a-half of making the decision that would change the rest of their lives.

Now with more than five years' experience living on the road, Natalie has cooked all across the country as well as in Baja, Mexico, Canada, and Alaska, in just about every landscape you can think of. She prides herself on creating community through food and deeply values the connections she has made. She shares her life journey on her Instagram account and YouTube channel, @letsplayrideandseek. There you can find excerpts from her travels, cooking videos, and recipes. Natalie's other love languages are writing poetry, losing herself in music, and digging her bare feet into whatever landscape she currently resides in.

Published in 2024 by Hardie Grant Explore,
an imprint of Hardie Grant Publishing

Hardie Grant Explore
(Melbourne)
Wurundjeri Country
Building 1, 658 Church Street
Richmond, Victoria 3121

Hardie Grant Explore
(Sydney)
Gadigal Country
Level 7, 45 Jones Street
Ultimo, NSW 2007

www.hardiegrant.com/au/explore

A catalogue record for this
book is available from the
National Library of Australia

Hardie Grant acknowledges the Traditional Owners of the
Country on which we work, the Wurundjeri People of the
Kulin Nation and the Gadigal People of the Eora Nation, and
recognises their continuing connection to the land, waters and
culture. We pay our respects to their Elders past and present.

For all relevant publications, Hardie Grant Explore
commissions a First Nations consultant to review relevant
content and provide feedback to ensure suitable language
and information is included in the final book. Hardie
Grant Explore also includes traditional place names and
acknowledges Traditional Owners, where possible, in both
the text and mapping for their publications.

Tiny Kitchen Feast
ISBN 9781741178814

10 9 8 7 6 5 4 3 2 1

Publisher Melissa Kayser
Project editor Megan Cuthbert
Editor Elen Turner
Proofreader Andrea O'Connor
Internal design Dian Holton
Cover design Celia Mance
Typesetting Hannah Schubert
Index Max McMaster
Production coordinator Simone Wall

Colour reproduction by Hannah Schubert and Splitting Image
Colour Studio

Printed and bound in China by LEO Paper Products LTD.

The paper this book is printed on is certified
against the Forest Stewardship Council®
Standards and other sources. FSC® promotes
environmentally responsible, socially beneficial
and economically viable management of the
world's forests.